Case Studies in Twentieth-Century History

Derek Heater

Longman
in association with the
Council for Education in World Citizenship
London and New York

Longman Group UK Limited,
Longman House, Burnt Mill, Harlow,
Essex CM20 2JE, England
and Associated Companies throughout the world.

Published in the United States of America
by Longman Inc., New York.

First published 1988
Second impression 1991

Set in 10/12 point Plantin
Produced by Longman Group (F.E.) Limited
Printed in Hong Kong

ISBN 0 582 34318 6

British Library Cataloguing in Publication Data
Heater, Derek
    Case studies in twentieth-century history.
    1. History, Modern — 20th century
    I. Title
    909.82   D421

    ISBN 0-582-34318-6

Library of Congress Cataloging-in-Publication Data
Heater, Derek Benjamin.
    Case studies in twentieth-century history/Derek Heater.
        p.   cm.
        Summary: Explores major modern issues such as international
    cooperation, war, and human rights through primary sources relating
    to specific incidents in twentieth-century history.
        ISBN 0-582-34318-6 : £3.95
        1. History, Modern – 20th century. 2. History, Modern – 20th
    century – Sources. [1. History, Modern – 20th century – Sources.]
    I. Title. II. Title: Case studies in 20th-century history.
    D421.H445 1988
    909.82 – dc 19

                                                    87-15755
                                                    CIP
                                                    AC

Contents

Acknowledgements

We are grateful to the following for permission to reproduce photographs: BBC Hulton Picture Library, page 78; Biafran Ministry of Information, page 111; Le Canard enchainé, page 22; Culver Pictures Inc, pages 84, 136; The *Daily Telegraph*, page 52; Fotomas Index, London, page 66; International Labour Office, page 128; The Keystone Collection, page 102; David King Collection, pages 59, 62; *New Statesman*, page 15; *The Observer*, page 18; Popperfoto, page 39; *Punch*, pages 11, 91; Solo Syndication & Literary Agency Ltd, page 29; *Sunday Observer*, page 19; *The Sunday Times*, page 144; Syndication International, page 48; Trades Union Congress, page 37 (photo: John Freeman & Co); The Wiener Library, page 122.

We are grateful to the following for permission to reproduce copyright material: table from F. Teer & J. D. Spence: *Political Opinion Polls*, 1973, Century Hutchinson Publishing Group Limited; chart from: R. A. Brady: *The Spirit and Structure of German Fascism*, 1937, Viking Penguin Inc and Otto Elsner Verlags-Gesell MBH & Co KG; bar graphs from The *Guardian* 23 June 1969; tables from *Factsheets on Britain and Europe*, No 9, June 1971, and *Management and Personnel Office, Public Bodies*, 1983, Controller of Her Britannic Majesty's Office; table from Organisation for Economic Co-operation & Development; two figures from Alan F. Sillitoe: *Britain in Figures: A Handbook of Social Statistics* (Penguin Books, 1971), copyright © Alan F. Sillitoe, 1971; figure from ed. Gwyn Prins: *Defended to Death* (Penguin Books, 1983), copyright © Penguin Books, 1983; table from M. Stacey & M. Price: *Women, Power and Politics*, Tavistock Publications, 1981; table from Uwe Kitzinger: *Diplomacy and Persuasion: How Britain Joined the Common Market*, Thames & Hudson Ltd, 1973; table from Adamthwaite: *The Making of the Second World War*, Unwin Hyman Ltd, 1977; table from The World Bank.

We are grateful to the following for permission to reproduce copyright material:
Associated Book Publishers (UK) Ltd for extracts from *Soviet Foreign Policy Since The Death of Stalin* by H. Hanak (pub. Routledge & Kegan Paul Plc, 1972); Cassell plc for an extract from *Triumph and Tragedy* by W. S. Churchill; the author, E. U. Essien-Udom and The University of Chicago Press for a letter from *Black Nationalism: The Rise of The Black Muslims in The USA* by E. U. Essien-Udom; Guardian Newspapers Ltd for extracts from articles by R. Clutterbuck in the *Guardian* 24/3/83 and P. Laurence in the *Guardian* 17/10/84 and 'Forgiving without forgetting' by J. De Haas in the *Guardian* 26/6/85; Hamlyn Publishing Group for a slightly adapted extract from *The World Crisis: The Aftermath* by W. S. Churchill; the Controller of Her Majesty's Stationery Office for extracts from the pamphlet *Britain and Europe* (1971); the Historical Society of Saratoga Springs, New York for an extract from *A Pearl in Every Oyster* by Frank Sullivan (1938); Macmillan Accounts and Administration Ltd and the author's agent for extracts from *A Rumour of War* by Philip Caputo; the author's agents for extracts from *Britain by Mass Observation* by Madge and Harrison; Mail Newspapers Ltd for an article by J. Blyth from the *Daily Mail* 5/11/56; the author's agent and Michael Joseph Ltd for an extract from *Goodbye Darkness* by William Manchester (1981); the Editor for a poem from the article 'Visions of the Return: The Palestine Refugees in Arabic Poetry and Art' by A. L. Tibawi in the *Middle East Journal* Autumn 1963; the Editor for an extract from the *Daily Worker* 5/11/56; The Observer Ltd for extracts from the *Observer* 20/6/76 and 6/1/85; Oxford University Press for an extract from *The Russian Revolution* by N. N. Sukhanov, trans. J. Carmichael (1955) and the poem 'Towering Aloft' by Mao Tse-Tung, trans. Michael Bullock and Jerome Ch'en from *Mao and The Chinese Revolution* by Jerome Ch'en (1965) © Oxford University Press 1965; Penguin Books Ltd for an extract from *The Palestinian Resistance* by Gerard Chaliand trans. Michael Perl (Penguin Books, 1972) Copyright © Gerard Chaliand 1972, translation Copyright © Michael Perl 1972; the author, Elie Siegmeister for extracts from his poem 'TVA Ballad' in *A Treasury of American Song* by Elie Siegmeister and Olin Downes, Copyright 1985, Music Copyright 1985 by Elie Siegmeister; St. Martin's Press, Inc and Allison & Busby, an imprint of W. H. Allen for extracts from *Hungary 1956* by B. Lomax (1976) Copyright Bill Lomax 1976; School Curriculum Development Committee Publications for sheet 662 'Prisoner on The Kwai' from *The Humanities Project: War & Society* (pub. Heinemann Educational Books for SCDC Publications, 1970); Times Newspapers Ltd for an extract from *The Times* 25/10/56.

We have been unable to trace the copyright holders in the following and would appreciate any information that would enable us to do so: a letter by J. F. Kennedy from *Kennedy* by T. C. Sorenson (1965); a letter from *British European* Vol 1, No. 3 April 1971; a short story cited in *Lord Russell: The Scourge of The Swastika* (1954 paperback edition pub. Corgi).

Foreword

For half a century the Council for Education in World Citizenship has helped pupils and teachers to comprehend major world events as they occurred. Distinguished academics, diplomats, politicians and journalists have written our current affairs broadsheets and spoken at our conferences. Always we have sought to analyse cause and effect with objectivity and to balance our platforms with speakers representing different points of view.

Over the years, CEWC has helped millions of young people in schools and colleges throughout the UK to weigh the evidence, read between the lines and come to their own conclusions on issues of the day.

Derek Heater's book is in the true CEWC tradition. Its purpose is to provide pupils with experience in using primary source material. Each topic is handled by the presentation of a range of sources: cartoons, photographs, extracts from speeches, newspapers and contemporary literature. The book has the advantage over CEWC's immediate response to current events in providing an historical perspective, so that the present can be interpreted through an understanding of the recent past.

The causes of international wars can only be understood through a knowledge of the ideologies and inequalities which divide states. Internecine conflict in Asia, the Middle East and Africa can only be understood in relation to the partition of India, Palestine and the End of Empire. Apartheid, anti-semitism, the troubles in Northern Ireland all derive from the denial of fundamental Human Rights. Peace and disarmament are not attainable through repetition or wishful thinking; they involve an understanding of the motivation of governments and the machinery of international co-operation.

This book is a valuable teaching and learning aid for those studying modern world history, politics, social studies or humanities, whether for GCSE or beyond. But it is first and foremost a book designed to help every young person come to terms with the perils and promise of an increasingly complex, dangerous and inter-dependent world and equip him or her to meet its challenges and opportunities.

We are grateful to Longman for responding to our initiative and to the author for bringing it to fruition.

MARGARET QUASS
COUNCIL FOR EDUCATION IN WORLD CITIZENSHIP
JUNE 1987

Preface

This book has been compiled with two purposes in mind: to provide a background for the study of five crucial issues in current world affairs; and to introduce students of History at GCSE and above to the task of handling primary sources in twentieth-century world history. In selecting the material an attempt has been made to provide as wide a coverage of topics and as diverse a range of sources as possible. Inevitably therefore some material, especially diplomatic documents, are couched in a less accessible style than others. However, it is hoped that this approach will render the book useful to a broad band of students' interests. Difficult words are printed in bold type and defined in a glossary at the end of each chapter.

Derek Heater

Part 1   International co-operation

Chapter 1   The Paris Peace Settlements: national self-determination

When the First World War came to an end many of the frontiers of Europe were changed and some new countries came into existence. The idea behind these changes was called 'national self-determination'. Many people at the time thought this was fair. But some thought that it could never work in practice.

Introduction

In the island of Britain frontiers mean less than they used to. England and Scotland ceased to be separate kingdoms in 1603. In the island of Ireland it is very different; the border between Northern and Southern Ireland was created in 1921. In Europe, by contrast, frontiers have been constantly redrawn over the centuries. And after each war statesmen have usually attended a conference to agree to re-drawing some of the frontiers between countries. The main principle which has guided these changes has been to take land from the defeated and to give it to the victors.

However, after the First World War the American President Woodrow Wilson introduced a different idea. This was the idea of national self-determination. He argued that people who thought of themselves as a nation should form a single state. For example, Poles should live in a

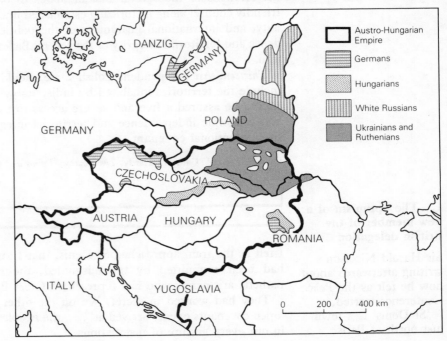

A Nationalities and boundaries in Central and Eastern Europe after the Paris Peace Settlements, 1921

The map shows the main minorities within the new frontiers, despite the policy of national self-determination.

Map legend:
- Austro-Hungarian Empire
- Germans
- Hungarians
- White Russians
- Ukrainians and Ruthenians

Countries shown: DANZIG, GERMANY, POLAND, CZECHOSLOVAKIA, GERMANY, AUSTRIA, HUNGARY, ROMANIA, ITALY, YUGOSLAVIA

0   200   400 km

country called Poland, which should be governed by Poles; and, as far as possible, there should be no other people inside Poland and no Poles outside Poland. Wilson believed that the war had broken out because before 1914 the frontiers of Europe were not drawn in this way. He also believed that only by changing frontiers would it be possible to prevent further wars. In addition, he believed that the various nationalities of Europe should decide for themselves where the frontiers should be. These ideas were expressed in his famous Fourteen Points.

There were, however, two major difficulties. One was that the French were afraid of Germany: they thought that national self-determination was much less important than keeping Germany weak. Secondly, as you can see from the map (Source A), the different nationalities of central Europe especially were scattered so that it was impossible to draw tidy boundaries between them.

Furthermore, President Wilson believed that a permanent international organisation should be created to deal peacefully with quarrels between states. This was the League of Nations. One of the tasks taken on by the League was to ensure that people who were a minority nationality in a state were treated fairly.

B   Some of President Woodrow Wilson's Fourteen Points, 1918

Nine. A readjustment of the frontiers of Italy should be **effected** along clearly recognizable lines of nationality.

Ten. The peoples of Austria-Hungary, whose place among the nations we wish to see safeguarded and assured, should be accorded the freest opportunity of **autonomous** development.

Eleven. Rumania, Serbia, and Montenegro should be evacuated, occupied territories restored, Serbia accorded free and secure access to the sea, and the relations of the several Balkan States to one another determined by friendly counsel along historically established lines of **allegiance** and nationality, and international guarantees of the political and economic independence and **territorial integrity** of the several Balkan States should be entered into. . . .

Thirteen. An independent Polish State should be erected which should include the territories inhabited by indisputably Polish populations, which should be assured a free and secure access to the sea, and whose political and economic independence and territorial integrity should be guaranteed by international **covenant**.

Quoted in G. M. Gathorne-Hardy, *The Fourteen Points and the Treaty of Versailles*, OUP, 1939.

C   The optimism of a new member of the British delegation

Sir Harold Nicolson writing afterwards about how he felt as the Peace Conference started.

'St Denis' is a town just north of Paris.

I felt as the train approached St Denis, that I knew exactly what mistakes had been committed by the misguided, the **reactionary**, the after all pathetic aristocrats who had represented Great Britain in 1814.

They had worked in secret. We on the other hand were committed to 'open covenants openly arrived at' . . . the peoples of the world would share in our every gesture of negotiations.

At Vienna again, they had believed in the doctrine of 'compensations'. . . . We believed in nationalism, we believed in the self-determination of peoples. 'Peoples and provinces', [Woodrow Wilson declared] . . . shall not be bartered about from **sovereignty** to sovereignty as if they were but **chattels** or pawns in the game. . . .

Nor was this all. We were journeying to Paris, not merely to **liquidate** the war, but to found a new order in Europe. We were preparing not peace only, but Eternal Peace. There was about us the halo of some divine mission.

Sir Harold Nicolson, *Peacemaking 1919*, Constable, 1933.

D The importance of geography and maps

Part of the Bowman Memorial Lecture, entitled 'Geography, Justice and Politics at the Paris Conference in 1919', which Charles Seymour, Head of the Austro-Hungarian Division of the US delegation at the Peace Conference, gave to the American Geographical Society in 1951.

'Bohemia' was part of Czechoslovakia and 'Masaryk' was President of Czechoslovakia.

For Wilson it was vital to know who the populations were whose freedom would be determined by new boundaries and how those boundaries would affect their emotional and their economic welfare. As he insisted, the wishes and needs of these peoples **transcended** everything else. For the other side it was of equal importance that these same facts should be at hand, in order clearly to determine the effect of new frontiers upon the balance of political interest.

Thus geography came into its own, and in the process of educating the statesmen it was fortunate that the necessary materials were at hand. . . . Mr. Wilson himself profited. . . . to his surprise, he learned that there was a great mass of Germans in northern Bohemia. 'Why', he said, 'Masaryk never told me that.'. . . Toward the end of the conference the statesmen's interest in and knowledge of maps was sufficient to guarantee a passing grade on a reasonably stiff examination.

Quoted in I. J. Lederer (ed.), *The Versailles Settlement – Was it Foredoomed to Failure?*, Heath & Co., 1960.

E Nationality defined by language

Winston Churchill describes afterwards the basis for self-determination.

All being agreed upon the fundamental principle [of self-determination], it remained to apply it. But if the principle was simple and accepted, its application was difficult and disputable. What was to be the test of nationality?. . .

In the main it was decided that language should be adopted as the proof of nationality. No doubt language is not always its **manifestation**. Some of the most nationally conscious **stocks** can scarcely speak their own language at all, or only with the greatest difficulty. Some oppressed races spoke the language of their oppressors, while hating them; and some dominant breeds spoke the language of their subjects, while ruling them. Still matters had to be settled with reasonable **dispatch**, and no better guide to the principle of nationality in disputed cases could be found than language; or, as a last resort, a **plebiscite**.

Nevertheless all . . . the disputable areas put together were but a minute fraction of Europe. They were but exceptions which proved the rule. . . . Probably less than 3 per cent of the European population are now living under Governments whose nationality they **repudiate**; and the map of Europe has for the first time been drawn in general harmony with the wishes of its peoples.

Winston Churchill, *The World Crisis: The Aftermath*, Odhams, 1929.

F   The views of Georges Clemenceau

The British economist, John Maynard Keynes, who attended the Peace Conference, describes Clemenceau's philosophy.

[Clemenceau's] philosophy had, therefore, no place for 'sentimentality' in international relations. Nations are real things, of which you love one and feel for the rest indifference – or hatred. The glory of the nation you love is a desirable end – but generally to be obtained at your neighbour's expense. The politics of power are inevitable, and there is nothing very new to learn about this war or the end it was fought for; England had destroyed, as in each preceding century, a trade rival; a mighty chapter had been closed in the **secular** struggle between the glories of Germany and of France. **Prudence** required some measure of lip service to the 'ideals' of foolish Americans and hypocritical Englishmen; but it would be stupid to believe that there is much room in the world, as it really is, for such affairs as the League of Nations, or any sense in the principle of self-determination except as an ingenious formula for rearranging the **balance of power** in one's own interests.

J. M. Keynes, *Essays in Biography*, Macmillan, 1933.

G   The punishment of Germany

(i) A warning written for the British Prime Minister, Lloyd George, by his private secretary in 1919.

You may strip Germany of her colonies, reduce her armaments to a mere police force and her navy to that of a fifth-rate power; all the same, in the end, if she feels that she has been unjustly treated in the peace of 1919, she will find means of exacting **retribution** from her conquerors. . . . injustice, arrogance displayed in the hour of triumph, will never be forgotten or forgiven.

For these reasons I am, therefore, strongly averse to transferring more Germans from German rule to the rule of some other nation than can possibly be helped.

Quoted in H. Elcock, *Portrait of a Decision: The Council of Four and the Treaty of Versailles*, Eyre Methuen, 1972.

(ii) Hitler condemns the acceptance of the Versailles Settlement in his book *Mein Kampf*.

What did our governments do to infuse into this nation once again the spirit of proud independence, manly defiance and national determination?

In 1919, when the German nation was burdened with the Peace Treaty, there was justification in hoping that that document of oppression would help on the cry for Germany's liberation. It happens sometimes that treaties of peace whose conditions beat upon a nation like **scourges** sound the first trumpet call for the **resurrection** which follows later.

How much might have been made out of the Treaty of Versailles!

Each point of it might have been burnt into the brains and feelings of the nation, till finally the common shame and the common hatred would have become a sea of flaming fire in the minds of sixty millions of men and women; out of the glowing mass a will of steel would have emerged, and a cry: We will be armed as others are armed!

Every opportunity was missed, and nothing was done. Who will wonder that our nation is not what it ought to be, and might be?

Adolf Hitler, *Mein Kampf*, 1925, Paternoster Library ed., 1933.

H Promises by the Czech Foreign Minister

Part of a list of promises sent by Edouard Beneš to the New States Committee, 20 May 1919.

8. The official language will be Czech, and this State will be known abroad as the Czecho-Slovak State, but in practice the German language shall be the second language of the country, and shall be employed currently in administration before the courts and in the central Parliament on an equal footing with Czech. It is the intention of the Czecho-Slovak Government to satisfy the population in practice and in daily use, but reserving a certain special position for the Czecho-Slovak language and element.

9. In other words, the present state would remain, only the German influence would be reduced to its just proportions.

10. It will be an extremely liberal regime, which will very much resemble that of Switzerland.

Quoted in C. A. Macartney, *National States and National Minorities*, OUP, 1934.

I The plebiscite in Upper Silesia

A British historian describes Lloyd George's views about the plebiscite.
    'Dr Lord' was Chief US Adviser on Poland.

Moving on to Upper Silesia, Wilson tried to argue that the difficulties involved in holding a plebiscite there were such as to render the idea impracticable. . . . To charges that the population would be intimidated, Lloyd George replied,

I know what it is to be oppressed and intimidated by great land-owners; I had experience of that in Wales, where one could make no appeal for outside help to throw off the yoke. In Upper Silesia the peasant population is small, and hence the number of people who can be thus intimidated is also small; most of the population of Upper Silesia are industrial workers, who are always difficult to intimidate.

The argument went on for some time along such lines as these, and in the end Lloyd George became exasperated at Wilson's persistent obstruction:

No-one has proclaimed more powerfully than you the right of people to decide their own fate. That means that the fate of peoples must be decided by the peoples themselves, and not by any Dr Lord who believes that he knows better than the people themselves what they want. I am doing nothing other than abiding by your Fourteen Points.

Elcock, *Portrait of a Decision*.

J   The League of Nations

The league persuaded several countries with 'minorities' to sign treaties promising to treat them well. This is an extract from the Polish treaty.

Article 2

Poland undertakes to assure full and complete protection of life and liberty to all inhabitants of Poland without distinction of birth, nationality, language, race or religion.

All inhabitants of Poland shall be entitled to the free exercise, whether public or private, of any creed, religion or belief, whose practices are not inconsistent with public order or public morals.

Article 8

Polish nationals who belong to racial, religious or linguistic minorities shall enjoy the same treatment and security in law and in fact as the other Polish nationals. In particular they shall have an equal right to establish, manage and control at their own expense charitable, religious and social institutions, schools and other educational establishments, with the right to use their own language and to exercise their religion freely therein.

Article 9

Poland will provide in the public educational system in towns and districts in which a considerable proportion of Polish nationals of other than Polish speech are resident adequate facilities for ensuring that in the primary schools the instruction shall be given to the children of such Polish nationals through the medium of their own language. This provision shall not prevent the Polish Government from making the teaching of the Polish language obligatory in the said schools.

Reprinted in Macartney, *National States and National Minorities*

Glossary

allegiance   loyalty and support (to a country)
autonomous   independent
balance of power   the balancing of rival strengths of different countries in international relations
chattels   movable property
covenant   agreement
dispatch   speed
effected   carried out
liquidate   end
manifestation   the way it is shown
plebiscite   vote by all the people
prudence   caution

reactionary   against change
repudiate   disown
resurrection   rebirth
retribution   a deserved punishment
scourges   causes of great suffering
secular   not connected with the church
sovereignty   freedom to govern independently
stocks   people
territorial integrity   no land shall be taken away
transcended   was more important than

Questions

1   (a)   By using Source A compile a list of countries wholly created from the former Austro-Hungarian Empire and another of countries which obtained land from that Empire.

(b)   Select three countries of central Europe shown on Source A. List the minority nationalities in each country, that is, people not of the same nationality as most of the population.

2   (a)   Compare Sources A and B. How far were points 9, 10, 11 and 13 in Source B put into effect?

(b)   What evidence is there in Source B that trade was as important a principle as nationality in the peace treaties?

3 What evidence is there in Source D that President Wilson had not thoroughly thought through the implications of his principle of self-determination?

4 Look at Source E.
   (a) List the problems of using language as the proof of nationality.
   (b) What does Churchill think about using language as the proof of nationality?

5 (a) Read Source C. What did Nicolson think were the main considerations which should be used as the basis of the peace settlement?
   (b) Read Source F. What did Clemenceau think were the main considerations which should be used as the basis of the peace settlement?
   (c) Would these two men have agreed or disagreed on these issues? Explain your answer.

6 Read Sources G(i) and (ii) and with the help of your own background knowledge decide whether each of the following statements is more likely to be true or false. Give the reasons for your decisions.
   (i) The Germans were guilty of causing the First World War and deserved to be punished.
   (ii) The peace settlement with Germany followed the principle of national self-determination and was very just.
   (iii) The German representatives signed the peace treaty too meekly in 1919. They should have asked for better terms.
   (iv) Lloyd George could have foreseen the popularity that a man like Hitler would gain from his attacks on the Versailles Settlement.

7 (a) Draw a sketch map of Czechoslovakia in 1921 showing where the German-speaking people lived.
   (b) What evidence is there in Source H that the frontier of Czechoslovakia was not drawn strictly according to the principle of nationality?

8 When frontiers are being redrawn should the people of the area decide for themselves to which country they shall belong? Use the evidence in Source I in your answer.

9 Explain how the statesmen at Paris in 1919 set about redrawing the frontiers of Europe so as to preserve the peace. Include in your answer the following words: *nationality; national self-determination; language; minorities; plebiscite.*

10 Read Source J. What right did the League of Nations have to interfere in this way in Poland's affairs?

Chapter 2 The United Nations: the peace-keeping operation in the Congo

One of the most difficult tasks the United Nations has had to deal with was the crisis in the Congo in 1960–61. Both the UN as a whole and its Secretary-General, Dag Hammarskjöld, were heavily criticised for the way they handled the crisis. Were these criticisms fair?

Introduction

Sixty million had been killed in two world wars; over 40 wars had been fought altogether. This was the dreadful arithmetic of conflict in the twentieth century by 1945, before it had run even half its course. And so in 1945 the countries of the world, horrified by the slaughter, set up the United Nations Organisation (UNO or UN as it is usually called). Its purpose was to maintain peace. One part of the UN, the Security Council, was to be responsible for taking action if a crisis developed which seemed to threaten world peace. The UN Charter (that is, the list of rules) also gave the Secretary-General authority to deal with dangers. From 1953 to 1961 the Secretary-General was the Swede, Dag Hammarskjöld, and he was especially active. During that time the UN was involved in one of the most difficult and controversial of its tasks – the crisis in the Congo.

The Congo (now called Zaïre) is a large country in the middle of Africa, and had been a Belgian colony for many years. In the 1950s some people, as in other African colonies, demanded freedom for their country. Suddenly, in 1959, the Belgian Government announced that the Congo was to be given independence. Yet the Belgians had done nothing to train the local people to take over the government. As a result, when the Belgians withdrew in 1960, the country collapsed into chaos.

These are the main events from 1960 to 1961 which you need to know in order to understand the sources.

1　June 1960: independence; Patrice Lumumba became prime minister.
2　July 1960: the army mutinied.
3　July 1960: the Congo Government appealed to the UN to restore order.
4　July 1960: Moise Tshombe declared Katanga a separate country. Katanga is a province in the south-east of the Congo. It has great mineral riches. The Belgians and some other Europeans hoped to keep control of the mines.
5　September 1960: Lumumba was dismissed as prime minister, but set up a rival government in the north-east province. Lumumba, a left-wing politician, was supported by the Russians.
6　January 1961: Lumumba was murdered by troops from Katanga.
7　September 1961: Hammarskjöld was killed in an air crash while flying to meet Tshombe for talks.

A Anarchy in the Congo

A journalist, working in the Congo, wrote this report for the *Daily Express* in 1960 after independence.

If this is freedom on the Congo, I have had enough of it.

For 11 days the Belgian Congo has been 'free' – now called the Independent Republic of the Congo.

And so far, short of wholesale murder, we have had nearly everything – revolution, rape, theft at the point of a bayonet, and mob rule.

The Belgian Government – by suddenly deciding to quit a country at least a generation away from being ready for self-government – asked for trouble, and certainly got it.

PEACE HOPES DASHED

There are still thousands of Europeans – including 10,000 missionaries – in the wild interior regions of the Congo. These people are in grave danger.

From the beginning I believed there could not be independence without trouble. A few days before 'freedom' day my hopes were rising that perhaps what seemed impossible might happen – that there would be independence and no trouble.

Thirty-four-year-old Prime Minister Patrice Lumumba, the man the Belgians tried not to have, finished off my hopes.

He got up and made a vicious, bitter speech against Belgian rule. In the first moments of the new country's life Lumumba sowed the seeds of hate from the past in the present.

It was an incitement to trouble – or worse.

From that moment on trouble was assured and the Congo will suffer more than the Belgians for it.

Daily Express, 11 July 1960.

B The Congo as an African problem

Dr Kwame Nkrumah was President of newly independent Ghana. He was speaking at the UN General Assembly, 23 September 1960.

It is quite clear that a desperate attempt is being made to create confusion in the Congo, extend the cold war to Africa, and involve Africa in the suicidal quarrels of foreign powers. The United Nations must not allow this to happen. We for our part will not allow this to happen. That is why we are anxious that the United Nations, having reached a point where intervention on the side of the **legitimate** Government of the Congo appears to be the obvious and only answer to this crisis, should act boldly through the **medium** of the independent African states.

Let these African states act under the canopy of the United Nations and produce the effective result. In these particular circumstances the Congo crisis should be handed over to the independent African states for solution. I am sure that, left to them, an effective solution can be found. It is negative to believe and hesitate until the situation becomes **irredeemable** and develops into another Korea.

Quoted in K. Nkrumah, *I Speak of Freedom*, Heinemann, 1961.

C The Soviet point of view

The Soviet leader, Nikita Khrushchev, writing to Jawaharlal Nehru, Prime Minister of India, 28 February 1961.
'Kasavubu' was the President of the Congo.

The slaughter of prime minister Lumumba and his comrades has exposed, for all the world to see, the disgusting role played in the Congolese events by United Nations secretary-general Hammarskjöld. The brutal murder of the outstanding leaders of the Congo Republic tragically demonstrated how **inadmissible** is the situation in which a **stooge** of the imperialists and colonialists heads the United Nations **executive machinery**.

It was none other than Hammarskjöld who **abetted** the seizure of prime minister Lumumba by bandits who had been handed their weapons by Belgium and other colonial states. Having entered into **collusion** with the colonialists, Hammarskjöld used his position as secretary-general in order to delay in every possible way the implementation of measures to protect the legitimate government and parliament of the Congo. Is it not significant that during his visit to the Congo Hammarskjöld negotiated with all and sundry, **kowtowed** to the puppets of the colonialists such as Kasavubu, Tshombe and others, but did not even want to meet Patrice Lumumba, the legitimate prime minister of the country, at whose request the troops of certain United Nations member states were sent to the Congo?

And when Patrice Lumumba and other statesmen were subjected to torture by the mercenary hangmen and it was obvious to the whole world that a vile assassination was being prepared, the United Nations secretary-general washed his hands of the whole affair and adopted a hypocritical pose of 'non-interference' . . . .

Such an individual has no right to hold a leading post in the United Nations.

Quoted in H. Hanak, *Soviet Foreign Policy since the Death of Stalin*, Routledge & Kegan Paul, 1972.

D Dag Hammarskjöld defends himself against Khrushchev's accusations

Hammarskjöld was speaking in the UN General Assembly, 3 October 1960.

The Head of the Soviet Delegation to the General Assembly, this morning, in exercising his right of reply, said, among many other things, that the present Secretary-General has always been biased against the socialist countries, that he has used the United Nations in support of the colonial Powers fighting the Congolese Government and Parliament in order to impose 'a new yoke on the Congo,' and finally, that if I, myself, and I quote, 'do not muster up enough courage to resign, so to say in a chivalrous manner, then the Soviet Union will draw the necessary conclusions from the **obtained situation.**'. . .

Let me say only this, that *you* all of you, are the judges. No single party can claim that authority. I am sure you will be guided by truth and justice. In particular, let those who know what the United Nations has done and is doing in the Congo, and those who are not pursuing aims proper only to themselves, pass judgement on our actions there. . . .

It is not the Soviet Union or, indeed, any other big Powers who need the United Nations for their protection; it is all the others. In this sense the Organization is first of all *their* Organization, and I deeply believe in the wisdom with which they will be able to use it and guide it. I shall remain in my post during the term of office as a servant of the Organization in the interests of all those other nations, as long as *they* wish me to do so.

Quoted in N. Gillett, *Dag Hammarskjöld*, Heron Books, 1970.

E Noah and the Congo Flood

Punch, 14 December 1960.

F Tshombe's point of view

Moise Tshombe, Prime Minister of Katanga, sent this telegram to Hammarskjöld on 27 October 1960.

The 'Mutiny of the *force publique*' was the refusal of the army to obey orders.

I am obliged to reject as unfounded your allegation that Katanga is threatening the **integrity** of the former Belgian Congo. Disintegration had already appeared in July 1960, at the time of the mutiny of the *force publique*. It was for that reason that I decided to proclaim Katanga's independence without delay, in order to protect my people from the chaos which was spreading through the former Belgian Congo as a result of the destructive activities of Lumumba and his **clique**. Immoderate **xenophobia** and recourse to the assistance of Communist countries precipitated further disorder and gave rise to **fratricidal** strife. It is to the excesses of the Central Government, headed by Lumumba, and not to Katanga, that responsibility for the collapse of the Republic of the Congo and for the subsequent tensions should be attributed.

Quoted in Royal Institute of International Affairs, *Documents on International Affairs*, OUP, 1960.

G   UN errors

The journalist Colin Legum, who has spent much of his time writing about Africa, describes what he sees as the errors of the UN in a book he wrote in 1961.

In retrospect it is much easier to see where the UN went wrong. It made three crucial errors all of which stem from the doctrine of 'non-intervention'. It made no effort to restore the unity of the Congo. It acted with equal impartiality towards the legal and the rebel governments. And it failed to deal effectively with the Force Publique. . . .

That 'non-intervention' was never possible is admitted even by the UN Organization for the Congo:. . .

The **fallacy** of the doctrine of 'non-intervention' in the Congo derives from the mistaken concept that the situation was **analogous** to previous interventions by the UN Force where, as a peace force, it could stop two **antagonists** getting at each other's throats. But this was not possible in the Congo, where the situation demanded active intervention on the side of the government.

Colin Legum, *Congo Disaster*, Penguin, 1961.

H   Praise for the UN operation

Hammarskjöld's biographer writes about the UN's involvement in 1961.

The 'take-off period' refers to the period just after independence in African countries.

'ONUC' are the initials of *Opération Nations Unies du Congo*, French for 'United Nations Operation in the Congo'. French is the European language spoken in the Congo.

The UN was on trial in Africa. Its newly independent countries were watching to see not only whether the UN could be relied upon to protect them from the cold war and give them disinterested help in the take-off period, but whether it would do so with a minimum of trespass on their newly gained **sovereignty**.

'For our part,' said President Bourguiba of Tunisia early in the ONUC operation, 'we have chosen to side with the UN.'

Nine months later, twenty African states . . . voted to stand firm behind UN efforts to achieve stability in the Congo and to advise all African states against interfering or taking sides with rival Congolese factions. They condemned all efforts to weaken the authority of the UN.

They knew by then that the UN's multi-national army of 20,000, along with a civilian operation of several hundred experts and administrators, had prevented civil war and kept the country afloat administratively and economically.

The Congo had developed into neither a Korea nor a Spain.

An international organization had again demonstrated the capacity to act. Hammarskjöld had kept faith.

The record in the Congo shows him and his colleagues to have been guided 'solely by the interest of the Congo and solely by the wish to develop the practices of this Organization in a way which may lay a foundation for future international co-operation.'

Joseph P. Lash, *Dag Hammarskjöld*, 1961, Cassell ed., 1962.

Glossary

abetted   helped
analogous   comparable with
antagonists   enemies
clique   a small group of people closed to outsiders
collusion   conspiracy
connivance   working together secretly
executive machinery   decision-making body
fallacy   false idea
fratricidal   literally brothers killing each other
inadmissible   unacceptable
In retrospect   with hindsight
integrity   independence
irredeemable   cannot be recovered
kowtowed   lamely took orders from
legitimate   legal
medium   method for giving information
obtained situation   what exists at the present time
sovereignty   independence
stooge   someone who does what other people want
xenophobia   hatred of foreigners

Questions

1   Whom does the *Daily Express* reporter in Source A blame for the chaos in the Congo? Using also your background knowledge, explain, with reasons, whether you think his view is completely fair.

2   Read Source B.
(a) Explain the following phrases: 'involve Africa in the suicidal quarrels of foreign powers'; 'another Korea'.
(b) What is Kwame Nkrumah's solution to the problem?

3   Read Source C and make a list of words and phrases which show Khrushchev's dislike of Hammarskjöld. Explain your choice.

4   Compare Sources C and D.
(a) What arguments does Hammarskjöld use to defend himself?
(b) Do you think his arguments would be likely to satisfy the Russians?

5   Look at Source E and explain what or who are represented by (a) Noah; (b) the Ark; (c) the water; (d) the animals; (e) the doves. Do you think that this is a fair summary of the problem? Explain your reasons.

6   Read Source F.
(a) Is it likely that this telegram contains the complete explanation for the break-away of Katanga? Explain the reasons for your answer.
(b) What other possible reasons for the break-away can you list? Why do you think they were omitted from the telegram?

7   (a) From the evidence in Sources G and H do you think that the UN operation in the Congo was more of a success than a failure? Explain the reasons for your conclusion.
(b) Explain how far you think these two sources are reliable as evidence on this matter.

Chapter 3 Arms control: nuclear arms negotiations

Since the 1950s many talks have been held and plans produced to try to stop the ever-increasing numbers of nuclear weapons. Yet all this effort has had almost no effect.

Introduction

In the summer of 1945 just two nuclear weapons existed – the atomic bombs which were dropped on Japan in August of that year. Forty years later there were about 55,000. Since 1945 there have been 'nuclear arms races'. The most important and serious has been between the USA and the USSR – an aspect of the Cold War between them. These two countries have come to fear each other so much that they feel their safety depends on a policy of nuclear deterrence. This means that each feels it must deter or prevent the other from making a nuclear attack by building up vast quantities of nuclear weapons. As a result, neither country will dare to strike first. For nuclear warfare would mean huge devastation and loss of life to both the attacker and the attacked.

However, there are powerful arguments against these stocks of nuclear bombs and missiles. If they are ever used, they would cause the most horrifying destruction of life over the whole planet. And there is always the fear that a nuclear war might break out accidentally. Moreover, although there has been no war between the USA and the USSR (perhaps because they have been deterred), each country has spent vast sums of money on the development of these weapons.

It is therefore not surprising that the two sides in the Cold War have made a number of attempts to reach agreements to reduce the dangers and to slow down the arms race.

A Eisenhower's scheme

President Dwight Eisenhower made this statement at the Geneva Summit Conference, 21 July 1955.

I should address myself for a moment principally to the delegates from the Soviet Union, because our two great countries admittedly possess new and terrible weapons in quantities which do give rise in other parts of the world, or **reciprocally**, to the fears and dangers of surprise attack.

I propose, therefore, that we take a practical step, that we begin an arrangement, very quickly, as between ourselves – immediately. These steps would include:

To give each other a complete **blueprint** of our military establishments. . . .

Next, to provide within our countries facilities for aerial photography to the other country . . . and by this step to convince the world that we are providing as between ourselves against the possibility of great surprise attack, thus lessening danger and relaxing tension.

Likewise we will make more easily attainable a comprehensive and effective system of inspection and disarmament, because what I propose, I assure you, would be but a beginning. . . .

The United States is ready to proceed in the study and testing of a reliable system of inspections and reporting, and when that system is proved, then to reduce armaments with all others to the extent that the system will provide assured results.

The successful working out of such a system would do much to develop the mutual confidence which will open wide the avenues of progress for all our peoples.

Quoted in R. J. Donovan, *Eisenhower: The Inside Story*, Hamish Hamilton, 1956.

B The nuclear arms race

New Statesman, 1960.

C The 'hot line'

President John Kennedy's close friend and adviser, Theodore Sorensen, describes the arrangement.

The 'teletype link' was a form of communication where messages were typed on a machine which was linked to a telephone line.

. . . the usual suspicions, misunderstandings and bureaucratic delays seemed destined at first to frustrate his hopes of converting the new atmosphere into any solid agreements. Only two minor accords were reached – the exchange of weather and other information from space satellites . . . and the 'hot line' teletype link between Moscow and Washington to make possible quick, private communications in times of emergency.

The 'hot line' – passing through Helsinki, Stockholm and London, but with no **kibitzers** – was not insignificant. Such a communications link . . . had been under discussion since Kennedy's first months in office; and its importance had been dramatized during the Cuban missile crisis when it had taken some four hours for the transmission of each Kennedy–Khrushchev message, including time for translation, coding, decoding and normal diplomatic presentation. . . . Khrushchev had made his final message of withdrawal public long before it had arrived in Washington as the only means of assuring its immediate delivery. A future crisis – which could be caused not only by some actual conflict but possibly by an accidental missile firing or some misleading indication of attack – might not permit either four hours or a public broadcast.

T. C. Sorenson, *Kennedy*, Hodder & Stoughton, 1965.

D The partial test-ban treaty

The Treaty Banning Nuclear-Weapon Tests in the Atmosphere, in Outer Space and Under Water was signed in Moscow, 5 August 1963.

The governments of the United Kingdom . . . , the Union of Soviet Socialist Republics, and the United States of America . . . have agreed as follows:

Article 1

Each of the Parties to this Treaty undertakes to prohibit, to prevent and not to carry out any nuclear test explosion, or any other nuclear explosion, at any place under its **jurisdiction** or control:

(a) in the atmosphere; beyond its limits, including outer space; or under water including **territorial waters** or high seas; or

(b) in any other environment if such explosion causes radioactive debris to be present outside the territorial limits of the state. . . . It is understood that the provisions of this sub-paragraph are **without prejudice** to the conclusion of a treaty resulting in the permanent banning of all nuclear test explosions, including all such explosions underground, the conclusion of which . . . the Parties . . . seek to achieve.

HMSO, 1963.

E Kennedy's point of view

An address by President Kennedy at the American University in Washington, 10 June 1963.

Some say that it is useless to speak of peace or world law or world disarmament – and that it will be useless until the leaders of the Soviet Union adopt a more **enlightened** attitude. I hope they do. I believe we can help them do it. But I also believe that we must re-examine our own attitude – as individuals and as a Nation – for our attitude is as essential as theirs.

. . . both the United States and its allies, and the Soviet Union and its allies, have a mutually deep interest in a just and genuine peace and in halting the arms race. Agreements to this end are in the interests of the Soviet Union as well as ours – and even the most hostile nations can be relied upon to accept and keep those treaty obligations, and only those treaty obligations, which are in their own interest.

So let us not be blind to our differences – but let us also direct attention to our common interests and the means by which those differences can be resolved. . . . For, in the final analysis, our most common link is that we all inhabit this small planet. We all breathe the same air. We all cherish our children's future. And we are all mortal.

Quoted in G. Prins (ed.), *Defended to Death*, Penguin, 1983.

F Soviet disarmament proposals

A Soviet writer comments on the attitude of the USA to Soviet proposals.

During the very first stage, the Soviet Union suggested withdrawing from armaments all **means of delivery**, stopping their production and destroying them, thus making it impossible from the beginning of disarmament for any country to attack another country with atomic or hydrogen weapons.

The U.S.A. and its allies rejected the Soviet proposal, alleging that they required some sort of additional guarantees for their security and had to retain a certain amount of delivery means even after the first stage of disarmament. But when the Soviet Government suggested that the U.S.S.R. and the U.S.A. retain an agreed limited number of rockets until disarmament is completed, the U.S.A. rejected this compromise proposal too.

O. Grinyov, 'Soviet Efforts for Disarmament' in the Moscow *International Affairs*, December 1967.

G Non-Proliferation Treaty (NPT) – the Soviet view

Premier Alexei Kosygin speaking at the signing of the Treaty on the Non-Proliferation of Nuclear Weapons, 1 July 1968.

Comrades, gentlemen, permit me, on the instructions of the Soviet government, to express profound satisfaction over the fact that the signing of the Treaty on the Non-**proliferation** of Nuclear Weapons, which is an important international document approved by the overwhelming majority of the UN members, starts today. The conclusion of a treaty of the non-proliferation of nuclear weapons is a major success for the cause of peace. Since the time nuclear weapons first appeared, the Soviet Union has firmly and consistently favoured delivering mankind from the nuclear threat. The Treaty is an important step towards this goal, since it bars the further spread of nuclear weapons, thus reducing the danger of an outbreak of a nuclear war.

The participation of a great number of states in the signing of the Treaty today is convincing proof that states are capable of finding mutually acceptable solutions to complicated international problems of vital importance for the whole of mankind. . . .

Quoted in H. Hanak, *Soviet Foreign Policy since the Death of Stalin*, Routledge & Kegan Paul, 1972.

H The 1960s arms race

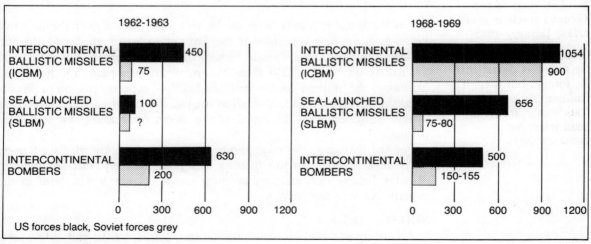

US forces black, Soviet forces grey

Guardian, 23 June 1969.

I The Strategic Arms Limitations Talks (SALT) treaties

(i) The terms of SALT I, 1972.

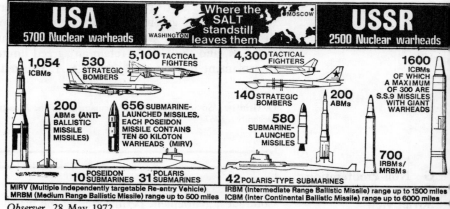

Observer, 28 May 1972.

(ii) The weaknesses of the SALT treaties.

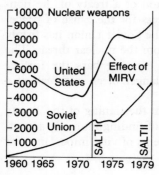

Source: CDI

The Strategic Arms Limitations Talks (SALT) have been represented to the public as extraordinarily complex and therefore lengthy discussions of highly technical matters. This is true. The SALT treaties have also been represented as being very important. In terms of stopping – or even slowing to any significant degree – the growth of the world's nuclear arsenal, this is not true, as can be seen from the rising curves in the graph of warhead numbers. Neither SALT I nor SALT II committed either superpower to surrender any weapon that it really wished to keep. In each case, the political price demanded by the respective military establishments and their **political lobbies** had the net effect of stimulating a further new twist in the upwards spiral of the arms race. These costs must be set against the international political benefit deemed to derive from the simple fact that the superpowers were at least talking to each other.

Prins, *Defended to Death*.

J The start of the Geneva nuclear arms talks, January 1985

'Schultz' was US Secretary of State, that is, foreign minister. The 'million buck-a-year "anchors"' are highly paid television commentators.

Given the bitter relations between the two superpowers over the past five years, even a mouse – perhaps in the form of an agreement for Shultz and Gromyko to meet again – would be something of a triumph. Yet with 1,000 journalists on hand – 200 from the powerful American TV networks, including the million-buck-a-year 'anchors' – expectations for a visible breakthrough are already sky-high as the two delegations arrive. Shultz was utterly dismayed when he heard of the media **razzmatazz** that had been planned.

For the Russians, the **megaphone effect** of the intense media attention on Geneva would seem to suit their new policies nicely. For observers in Moscow believe that what we are now seeing is quite a new **feint** in the superpower wrestling match.

SHOALS AHEAD

According to them, Moscow's refusal to talk had, by the end of last year, been judged counter-productive by the Kremlin. By returning to talks, the

Russians give themselves a much better opportunity to exploit their auxiliary weapon – a massive propaganda campaign against space weapons which will use both **malleable** Western Communist parties, all segments of Western peace movements, plus the sympathetic parts of the Western establishments.

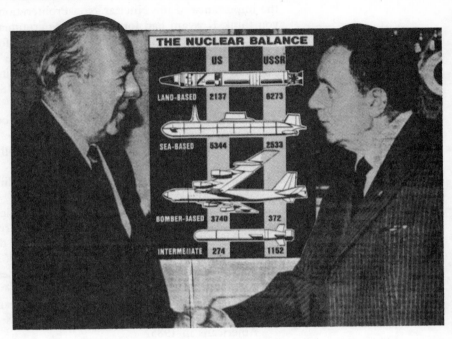

Observer, 6 January 1985.

Glossary

blueprint plan
Cold War tension between countries but without actual fighting
enlightened having complete understanding
feint an action to draw the enemy's attention from the real danger
jurisdiction power, held by an official body
kibitzers opportunities for people to intercept messages
malleable that which can be moulded and therefore controlled

means of delivery aircraft and missiles
megaphone effect increasing the noise and therefore publicity
political lobbies politicians who unite for or against a specific action
proliferation spread
razzmatazz noisy, colourful occasion
reciprocally between each other
territorial waters the sea near a country's coast, where its laws apply
without prejudice will not affect

Questions

1 Look at Source B. Then (a) name the four runners; (b) explain the letters on their torches; (c) explain the meaning of the flag.
2 Read Source C. Why was the 'hot line' set up?
3 Read Source D.
   (a) What kind of tests are still allowed by the treaty?
   (b) Why was it thought to be important to try to ban tests?

4   Read Source F and using other relevant information answer the following questions.

(a) Why, according to the USSR, did the USA reject the treaty?

(b) What other reasons were there for rejection?

5   Read Source G and write in your own words the reasons Kosygin gives for the importance of the Nuclear Non-Proliferation Treaty. What motives do you think Kosygin had for giving these arguments?

6   Look at Source H and say whether each of the following statements is more likely to be true or false. Give reasons for your decisions.

(i) The USA had to build rockets quickly in the 1960s because when Kennedy became President in 1961 the USA suffered from a 'missile gap' with the USSR.

(ii) Khrushchev sent missiles to Cuba in 1962 because of American superiority at that time.

(iii) Both the USA and the USSR increased all their means of delivering nuclear weapons during the 1960s.

(iv) During the 1960s the Soviets were building ICBMs faster than the Americans.

7   Look at Sources I(i) and (ii) and explain in which ways the Americans and in which ways the Soviets had advantages as a result of the SALT I treaty.

8   From the evidence in Sources H, I(i) and J draw a graph showing the numbers of (a) US and (b) Soviet ICBMs in 1963, 1965, 1969, 1972, 1985.

(a) When did the Americans have four times the number of ICBMs compared with the Soviets?

(b) When did the Soviets overtake the Americans in numbers of ICBMs?

(c) How many more ICBMs did the Soviets have compared with the Americans in 1985?

9   Compare Sources A, E and J. What evidence do they provide of the obstacles to agreement between the two superpowers on nuclear disarmament? Why had the difficulties increased from 1955 to 1985?

10   Have the governments of the USA and USSR always been sincere in saying they want agreements over nuclear weapons? Give reasons for your answer by referring to the sources which provide the best evidence for your purpose.

Chapter 4 The European Community: British entry

It was not until sixteen years after its creation that Britain joined the Common Market. What were the arguments for and against Britain's membership?

Introduction

Is it a good idea for countries to lose some of their independence and join together? After the Second World War various schemes were produced to increase co-operation among the countries of Western Europe. In 1952 six countries took a particularly important step by creating the European Coal and Steel Community (ECSC). These countries were: Belgium, France, Italy, Luxembourg, the Netherlands and West Germany. When the negotiations for the ECSC had started, in 1950, Britain was invited to join, but refused.

In 1957 the Six, as they came to be called, extended their co-operation by creating also the European Economic Community (EEC or the Common Market) and the European Atomic Energy Authority (Euratom). Again, Britain remained apart, and instead of joining, created the rival, but looser, European Free Trade Association (EFTA).

There were many reasons why Britain was at first reluctant to join with her west European neighbours in creating what has come to be called the European Community (sometimes also called the European Communities, or, simply, the Common Market). First, as an island, with its own traditions, Britain felt rather different from the countries of the Six. Secondly, she had special ties with both the USA and the member-countries of the Commonwealth; and was worried that these would be weakened if she became a member of the European Community. Thirdly, she was suspicious of the powers of the 'Eurocrats' – the civil servants who draw up the various regulations of the Community.

However, by about 1960 an increasing number of people in Britain saw that the Six were becoming quite wealthy and that perhaps it had been a mistake for Britain to remain outside the Community.

A De Gaulle's veto

General Charles de Gaulle, President of France, opposing Britain's application to join the Common Market, 14 January 1963.

Britain is, in fact, **insular** and maritime, linked by her trade, her markets, and her supply routes to very varied and often very remote countries. She is entirely industrial and commercial: hardly agricultural at all.

In her daily life, her habits and traditions are very special and very original. In short, the structure and present condition of England are widely different from those on the continent.

How can things be arranged so that Britain, living, producing and trading as she does, can still be incorporated into the Common Market as the latter has been conceived and functions? For example, the method by which Britain receives her food supply, which is to import supplies bought at the lowest prices from the two Americas and the old Dominions, while at the same time giving big **subsidies** to the peasants in England, is obviously incompatible with the system which the Six have naturally established among themselves.

It might have been thought that our English friends, in proposing their entry, had agreed to transform themselves to the point where they could apply all the required conditions.

The question today is whether they can accept coming inside a single tariff wall, renouncing all preferences for the Commonwealth, abandoning any privileges for their own farmers, and **repudiating** the pledges they made to their EFTA partners. This is the real question.

It cannot be said that at the present time Britain is ready to do these things. Will she ever be? To that question only Britain can reply.

Quoted in N. Beloff, *The General Says No*, Penguin, 1963.

B   A French cartoonist's view of Britain and the Europe of the Six

The hope of recovery

Le Canard enchaîné, 18 October 1967.

C   Arguments against British membership

Douglas Jay, a Labour MP and President of the Board of Trade, 1964–67, puts the arguments against membership.

Neither economically, politically, culturally nor sentimentally are we merely a European power – if indeed 'Europe' can be said to exist as anything more than a stretch of land from the Urals to the Atlantic coast. The British public just does not feel itself more closely allied to Poles or Spaniards than to the people of Australia or New Zealand.

There are, in any case, two overriding reasons why, if we are to survive, our world links, and our ties with continents other than Europe, must be preserved and fostered. First, much the greater part of our trade and investment overseas is conducted with countries outside Europe. Not merely, however, is a major part of our trade thus carried on with other continents, but an even higher proportion – very nearly the whole – of our really essential imports come from outside Europe also. Of the commodities which we must have in order to live – grain, meat, dairy produce, sugar, tea, coffee, oil, metals, wool, cotton, rubber and timber – the great bulk comes from outside Europe; mainly from North America, Australia, New Zealand, India and Pakistan, Africa, the Middle East, the West Indies and Malaya. Iron ore and timber from Scandinavia are almost Britain's only essential import from Western Europe; and these we could if necessary buy elsewhere. . . .

Secondly, Britain's closest political and human links have been for generations, and still are, with those nations which were largely created by British emigration, capital, and economic development over the last two centuries.

Douglas Jay, *After the Common Market: A Better Alternative for Britain*, Penguin, 1968.

D A persuasive front page?

British European, vol. 1, no. 6, July–August 1971.

E The British Government tries to persuade the public

This pamphlet was issued by the government in 1971.

A 'White Paper' is an official pamphlet announcing and explaining a government's policy on a particular matter.

THE OPPORTUNITY
The price we shall have to pay for the economic and political advantages of joining the Community has been set out in this short version of the Government White Paper. These advantages will more than outweigh the costs, provided we seize the opportunities of the far wider home market now open to us.

Higher standards of living
If we do as the Six members of the Community have done, then we shall get a substantial increase in our trade and a stimulus to growth and investment. We shall also get a greater rise in real wages and standards of living than we have known for years or than would be possible if we remained outside. . . .

An influence in the world
We have grown accustomed to the political and military predominance in the world of the two super powers, the United States and Russia. In economic affairs the Community and Japan are well on their way to super power status. These giants will increasingly set the pattern of economic life.

If we join, we should have more opportunity and strength to influence events than we could possibly have on our own; if we do not join, the Community would continue to grow in strength without us. Our power to influence the Community would steadily diminish while the Community's power to influence us would as steadily increase.

Britain and Europe
Together we could tackle the problems of technological development which would be far too big for any one of us.
Together we could compete more effectively overseas.
Together we could help the poorer countries of the world more generously than if we were working on our own.
For the first time since the war a Europe united would have the means of recovering the position in the world which Europe divided has lost.

Britain & Europe – pamphlet issued by HM Government, HMSO, 1971.

F   An argument against the government's White Paper

The *New Statesman*, a left-wing journal, published this pamphlet in 1971 as an answer to the government's White Paper.

The costs of joining the Community . . . would depress our living standards and threaten employment, would immeasurably outweigh any advantage that can be expected. It would be sheer **escapism** and an act of gross irresponsibility for the Government to enter the Common Market, with this prospect in view, simply because there are problems of economic management which have not yet been solved or because in recent years our economic performance has been below our expectations.

Beyond these economic considerations are the broad political perspectives. Outside the Community we can better serve our own interests and those of our traditional friends and allies. In many spheres we can, as we do already, combine with the Community in joint endeavours. . . .

The choice for Britain is clear. Either we maintain our existing freedom, our close and valued associations overseas and join with others in shaping those world policies and institutions that are needed in the years ahead not just by the people of one half of a continent but by all mankind, or we choose against the strong current of our interests and sentiments to enter the European Community and to join there in an exclusively continental association, doomed to strive for a unity and a power which will always be beyond its reach.

'The Case Against Entry: The United Kingdom and the European Communities', *New Statesman*, 1971.

G   A comparison of British export figures

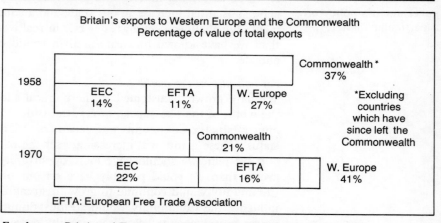

EFTA: European Free Trade Association

Factsheets on Britain and Europe, issued by HM Government, no. 9, June 1971.

H Comparisons of standards of living

The 'ECSO' is the Statistical Office of the European Communities and 'OECD' is the Organisation for Economic Co-operation and Development.

The 'Commission' is the civil servants of the European Communities.

(i) Trends in wages and living costs 1964 = 100

	Consumer price index 1973	Hourly gross wages index 1973	Real rise in wages %
Belgium	147	242	65
France	152	239	57
Germany	138	210	52
Italy	148	266	80
Luxembourg	140	200	73
Netherlands	170	254	79
UK	168	233[1]	39
Denmark	173[2]	242[2]	40
Ireland	179	296	65
USA	143	161	13

[1] *Adult men only*
[2] *1972*
Source: ECSO

(ii) Consumers' durables (numbers in use per 1,000 population – 1972)

	Cars	TV sets	Telephones
Belgium	219	216	224
France	256	227	185
Germany	253	299	249
Italy	207	191	188
Luxembourg	291	209	346
Netherlands	220	243	280
Six	237	227	217
UK	222	298	289
Denmark	228	277	356
Ireland	140	164	109
Nine	232	242	235
USA	432	399	567
Japan	86	214	194

Sources: ECSO, OECD

The Common Market and the Common Good, published on behalf of the Commission of the European Communities, Brussels, not dated but 1975.

I The results of the public opinion polls

(i) Changes in the views of the British people, 1966–72.

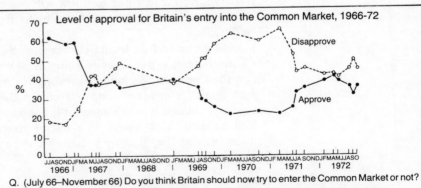

Level of approval for Britain's entry into the Common Market, 1966-72

Q. (July 66–November 66) Do you think Britain should now try to enter the Common Market or not?

Q. (February 67–January 69) Do you approve or disapprove of the Government's decision to try and join the Common Market?

Q. (July 69–Oct 72) Do you approve or disapprove of Britain joining the Common Market?

F. Teer and J. D. Spence, *Political Opinion Polls*, Hutchinson, 1973.

(ii) Attitudes in Britain and the Common Market countries about Britain joining, 1970.

	In favour	Against %	Don't know
EEC	64	8	28
Holland	79	8	13
Luxembourg	70	6	24
West Germany	69	7	24
France	66	11	23
Belgium	63	8	29
Italy	51	9	40
Britain	19	63	18

Uwe Kitzinger, *Diplomacy and Persuasion: How Britain Joined the Common Market*, Thames & Hudson, 1973, reporting a poll conducted by the EEC.

J   The concerns of ordinary people

(i) A fruit grower from Dover and Deal expresses his opposition at the Conservative Party Conference in October 1971.

How the hell I am going to take a lower price for my fruit and vegetables I'm damned if I know. . . . If we join Europe and throw away half our trade with the southern hemisphere, we'll be handing it over to the little yellow Nips – and I'm no brother to them. Some of you are brothers to all, but I'm not. I'm not pro-European, I'm not pro-Commonwealth. I'm pro-English, and I think it's about time we all were.

Quoted in Kitzinger, *Diplomacy and Persuasion*.

(ii) Marjorie Proops, well-known columnist for the *Daily Mirror*, answers women's questions.

Dear Marje,
    Everyone I hear talking about the Common Market seems to know what it's all about and I suppose, after everything that's been said and written about it, I should know, too.
    But frankly, I'd just like to know why we're going into it at all?
                                                        Mrs. Phyllis P.
Dear Phyllis,
    I could go on and on listing the reasons, but to be brief and factual and not bore the ears off you, we're going in so we can share in the prosperity which the Common Market is providing for its present member countries.
    And don't let anyone argue you out of the certainty that it *will* mean prosperity, though it won't mean it'll happen the day after we join.
    You have to think ahead, to think of your children and their children and the benefits they'll enjoy because we were sensible enough to plan now for a better future for everyone.

British European, Vol. 1, no. 3, April 1971.

Glossary

escapism   not facing up to reality
insular   of an island
manifesto   statement of intentions by a political party

repudiating   refusing to have anything to do with
subsidies   financial help

Questions

1   Read Source A and explain the meaning of the following: 'the Old Dominions'; 'the Six'; 'tariff wall'; 'EFTA'.

2   Study Sources A, B and C.
   (a) What are General de Gaulle's reasons for opposing Britain's entry into the Common Market?
   (b) What arguments are given in Source C against Britain's entry?
   (c) In what ways does Source C support Source A?
   (d) In the light of Source C, would you say that Source B was justified?

3   Look at Source D.
   (a) What propaganda methods are used here to persuade the British public that Britain should join the Common Market?
   (b) Explain, with reasons, whether you think these methods would have been effective.

4   From the evidence in Sources E and F draw up a table of arguments for and against British entry into the Common Market in 1971. Why do you think that the British Government believed that the arguments in favour were stronger than the arguments against?

5   Study Source G and write an imaginary speech based on this evidence in favour of Britain's entry into the Common Market.

6   What evidence is there in Source H that Britain had a lower standard of living in the early 1970s than the original six members of the Common Market?

7   Study Sources I(i) and (ii) and, using your own knowledge also, decide whether each of the following statements is true or false. Give your reasons.
   (i) When Edward Heath became prime minister and decided to open negotiations for British membership of the Common Market, public support for membership was at its lowest ebb.
   (ii) Only a year after General de Gaulle's resignation a larger proportion of French people than the average for the EEC as a whole wished Britain to join the Community.
   (iii) Only a minority of the British public approved of British membership when Mr Heath signed the Treaty of Accession making Britain a member.

8   Read Sources E, J(i) and J(ii) and write an imaginary reply by Marjorie Proops to the fruit-grower. Explain whether you think he would be convinced by the arguments.

Part 2   War

Chapter 5   The origins of the Second World War: Europe 1937–39

There has been a great deal of controversy, both at the time and since, about how the British and French Governments dealt with Hitler. Could they have done more to prevent the outbreak of the Second World War?

Introduction

How do you deal with bullies? Should you stand up to them and fight however much you might get hurt yourself? Or should you give in, at least a little, for fear of being beaten up? This was the dilemma facing the governments of Britain and France in the 1930s as Mussolini and Hitler built up their armed forces and demanded extra land for their countries. People in Britain and France still had vivid memories of the dreadful slaughter of the First World War and did not want to risk another one. Some people also felt that what Mussolini and Hitler wanted was really quite reasonable.

At first, the British Government believed that they could stop the dictators from bullying too much by persuading them to sign treaties. Then, some politicians, in particular the British Prime Minister, Neville Chamberlain, tried 'appeasement'. This meant giving in to some of the dictators' demands, expecting that they would then be satisfied.

The way this policy of appeasement was tried and failed is a complicated story. The extracts in this section therefore concentrate only on the period November 1937 to February 1939. The autumn of 1938 was particularly important. Hitler threatened Czechoslovakia because of the supposed discrimination against the German-speaking people there. Chamberlain met Hitler three times to try to prevent war from breaking out over this quarrel. The third meeting was held at Munich and also involved France and Italy. An agreement was signed. Chamberlain believed that he had preserved peace.

A Hitler describes his plans for war

Colonel Hossbach wrote the minutes of a meeting between Hitler and his senior commanders which took place on 10 November 1937.

The Führer then continued:

The aim of German policy was to make secure and to preserve the racial community and to enlarge it. It was therefore a question of space. . . .

German policy had to reckon with two hate-inspired **antagonists**, Britain and France, to whom a German **colossus** in the centre of Europe was a thorn in the flesh, and both countries were opposed to any further strengthening of Germany's position either in Europe or overseas; in support of this opposition they were able to count on the agreement of all their political parties. Both countries saw in the establishment of German military bases overseas a threat to their own communications, a safeguarding of German commerce, and, as a consequence, a strengthening of Germany's position in Europe. . . .

Germany's problem could only be solved by means of force and this was never without attendant risk. . . .

If the Führer was still living, it was his unalterable resolve to solve Germany's problem of space at the latest by 1943–45.

Quoted in A. P. Adamthwaite (ed.) *The Making of the Second World War*, Allen & Unwin, 1977.

B Military strengths

(i) Numbers of army divisions.

Table 1 Numbers of army divisions

	January 1938	*August 1939*
Germany	81	120–30
Italy	73	73
France	63	86
Great Britain	2	4

(ii) Numbers of warplanes.

Table 2 Numbers of warplanes

	January 1938	*August 1939*
Germany	1,820	4,210
Italy	1,301	1,531
France	1,195	1,234
Great Britain	1,053	1,750

Adamthwaite, *The Making of the Second World War*.

C 'The Autograph Collector'

This cartoon by David Low criticises Britain's faith in treaties with the dictators.

Evening Standard, 1933.

D   British and French public opinion

A leading French journalist, writing in 1938, explains the British and French attitude to the threat of war.

. . . The attitude is much the same in both countries [Great Britain and France], but the reasons for it are quite different. In France, war is not feared, but hated. Public opinion takes the point of view that war, which may perhaps be inevitable, would involve the utter ruin of our civilization. Hence what must be done at any cost is to gain time by favouring every possible concession. At all events, before taking the final step which would result in a ghastly conflict, the government must convince the French people that every attempt had been made to avoid war. If, however, war should come, there is not a Frenchman, whatever his political party may be, who would oppose a government which had made every effort to ward off the catastrophe. . . .

In Great Britain the blackmail exercised by Germany and Italy produces different effects. The profound belief in the strength of the British Empire which is cherished by every Englishman, whatever class he may belong to, convinces him that under no circumstances can anything ever happen to the Empire. No Englishman has the slightest doubt that all nonsense will stop as soon as Great Britain makes up her mind to stop it. Hence it is with a superior smile that the average Englishman watches Italy meddling on so many fronts at the same time.

Geneviève Tabouis, *Blackmail or War*, Penguin, 1938.

E   Adolf Hitler's order for the destruction of Czechoslovakia, 30 May 1938

1) *Political Assumptions*.
It is my unalterable decision to smash Czechoslovakia by military action in the near future. . . .

An unavoidable development of events within Czechoslovakia, or other political events in Europe providing a suddenly favourable opportunity which may never recur, may cause me to take early action. . . .

. . . To this end preparations are to be made immediately.
2) *Political Possibilities for Commencing the Operation*.
The following are necessary **prerequisites** for the intended attack:
a) A convenient apparent excuse and, with it,
b) Adequate political justification,
c) Action not expected by the enemy which will find·him in the least possible state of readiness.

Most favourable from a military as well as a political point of view would be lightning action as the result of an incident which would subject Germany to unbearable **provocation**, and which, in the eyes of at least a part of world opinion, affords the moral justification for military measures.

Moreover, any period of diplomatic tension prior to war must be terminated by sudden action on our part, unexpected in both timing and extent, before the enemy is so far advanced in his state of military readiness that he cannot be overtaken.

Quoted in Adamthwaite, *The Making of the Second World War*.

F Winston Churchill's view of the Munich Agreement

Part of Churchill's speech in the House of Commons, 5 October 1938.

I do not grudge our loyal, brave people, who were ready to do their duty no matter what the cost, who never flinched under the strain of last week – I do not grudge them the natural, spontaneous outburst of joy and relief when they learned that the hard ordeal would no longer be required of them at the moment; but they should know the truth. They should know that there has been gross neglect and deficiency in our defences; they should know that we have sustained a defeat without a war, the consequences of which will travel far with us along our road; they should know that we have passed an awful milestone in our history, when the whole **equilibrium** of Europe has been **deranged**, and that the terrible words have for the time being been pronounced against the Western democracies: 'Thou art weighed in the balance and found wanting.' And do not suppose that this is the end. This is only the beginning of the reckoning. This is only the first sip, the first foretaste of a bitter cup which will be **proffered** to us year by year unless by a supreme recovery of moral health and **martial vigour**, we arise again and take our stand for freedom as in the olden time.

Quoted in W. S. Churchill, *Into Battle*, Cassell, 1941.

G Reactions of the British public to the Munich agreement

Bus Conductor, age 30, Lewisham. 'I should think they should reject them. What the hell's he got the right to go over there and do a dirty trick like that? It'll have the whole world against us now. Who'll trust us? It's like throwing your own kid to the wolves. We helped make it a country and then Chamberlain comes along and wants to buy that swine off. There'll be a war sooner or later, and then there'll be nobody to help us. America won't lend us a bloody cent then. It's a cert if they've any guts they'll not give in.'

Woman, aged 32, in Whitehall. Lives in Pimlico. 'It's not fair. At first I thought it was all right. Now it seems it's a low-down dirty deal. He might have given them the chance to say what they were prepared to do. It gives lots of them Czechs over to Hitler now for him to pay out as he likes and won't he just do it if we know anything. . . . I think people are changing round now, they thought last week that it looked like peace. Now it looks as if he is going to get everything he wants because everybody is frightened to stop him.'

1. *Woman of 60.* 'Prime Minister a brave man and a good one. Perhaps war must come.' But her son, aged 30, said: 'Prime Minister has betrayed Czechs.'
4. *Woman of 30.* 'If we knew more about it we could form an opinion. Chamberlain did a grand thing. Best thing is to forget all about it. . . .
12. *Man of 40.* 'What'll he want to get away with next, I think, where's he going to stop? Chamberlain's making us stink in the eyes of the world.'

C. Madge and T. Harrisson, *Britain by Mass Observation*, Penguin, 1939.

H   Minutes of the British Cabinet meeting, 31 October 1938

The 'Dictator Powers' were Germany and Italy.

THE PRIME MINISTER said that he would speak next day when the House re-assembled and he would have to deal with foreign policy, both generally and in relation to our rearmament programme.

Our Foreign policy was one of **appeasement**: We must aim at establishing relations with the Dictator Powers which will lead to a settlement in Europe and to a sense of stability.

There had been a good deal of talk in the country and in the Press about the need for rearmament by this country. In Germany and Italy it was suspected that this rearmament was directed against them, and it was important that we should not encourage these suspicions.

The Prime Minister said that he proposed to make it clear that our rearmament was directed to securing our own safety and not for purposes of aggression against other countries.

A good deal of false emphasis had been placed on rearmament, as though one result of the Munich Agreement had been that it would be necessary for us to add to our rearmament programmes. Acceleration of existing programmes was one thing, but increases in the scope of our programme which would lead to a new arms race was a different proposition.

Quoted in Adamthwaite, *The Making of the Second World War.*

Glossary

antagonists   countries opposed to each other
appeasement   the idea of achieving peace by giving the enemy what he wants
colossus   huge figure
deranged   disturbed

equilibrium   balance
martial vigour   soldierly strength
prerequisites   conditions prevailing before the event
proffered   offered
provocation   reason for being made angry

Questions

1   Read Sources A and E.
   (a) What do they tell you about Hitler's attitude towards war?
   (b) How reliable do you think these sources are as evidence of Hitler's views?
   (c) What other evidence is there in this section that Hitler was preparing for war?

2   (a) What evidence is there in Source B to suggest that the Axis Powers were relatively stronger than Britain and France on the eve of war than at the beginning of 1938?
   (b) From your own knowledge explain why Britain had such a small army in the 1930s compared with other major European countries.

3   Name the three main men represented in Source C. What does the cartoon say about the policy of appeasement?

4   Look at Sources D and G. Which do you consider offers the most reliable view of British public opinion? Give reasons for your answer.

5   How far do Sources F and G support or contradict the view of the British public expressed in Source D?

6   Read Sources F, G and H. Which members of the public who were interviewed agree most closely with Churchill and which with Chamberlain? Explain the reasons for your choice.

7   What evidence can you find in these sources to show a deep level of distrust between Britain and France?

Chapter 6 The Second World War: the Far East and Pacific

In the study of the Second World War the conflict in the Far East and the Pacific is often given less emphasis than the war in Europe. How important was the war against Japan?

Introduction

Was the Second World War one war or two wars? In many ways it is helpful to study the Second World War as if it were two: one in Europe, the Atlantic and the Middle East; the other in the Far East and the Pacific. In the Far East Japan was fighting against the USA, Britain, including her Indian Empire, and China. Russia was not involved until the very end. The geography of the area created special difficulties. In particular, the American and British forces were not used to fighting in the jungle conditions of the Pacific islands and Burma.

The Japanese Government started the war because they wished to control the western Pacific area of the world and felt that the Americans were rivals there. Neither the Americans nor the British were prepared for such a war and they both suffered serious defeats at first. The Japanese captured so much of south-east Asia and the Pacific in 1941–42 that the Allies had a huge task to recapture all this land. The task was especially difficult because the Japanese forces fought very heroically with little fear of death. Furthermore, the Allied commanders in these areas were kept short of men and supplies because Roosevelt and Churchill agreed to concentrate on defeating Germany first.

A Japan's surprise attack on the USA

President Franklin Roosevelt requests Congress to declare war on Japan, 8 December 1941.
'Oahu' was the site of the US naval base of Pearl Harbor on one of the Hawaiian islands. Hawaii is a group of islands in the Pacific Ocean, now one of the states of the USA.

To the Congress of the United States:

Yesterday, December 7, 1941 – a date which will live in **infamy** – the United States of America was suddenly and deliberately attacked by naval and air forces of the Empire of Japan.

The United States was at peace with that Nation and, at the **solicitation** of Japan, was still in conversation with its Government and its Emperor looking toward the maintenance of peace in the Pacific. Indeed, one hour after Japanese air squadrons had commenced bombing in Oahu, the Japanese Ambassador to the United States and his colleague delivered to the Secretary of State a formal reply to a recent American message. While this reply stated that it seemed useless to continue the existing diplomatic negotiations, it contained no threat or hint of war or armed attack.

It will be recorded that the distance of Hawaii from Japan makes it obvious that the attack was deliberately planned many days or even weeks ago. During the intervening time the Japanese Government has deliberately sought to deceive the United States by false statements and expressions of hope for continued peace.

Quoted in H. A. Jacobsen and A. L. Smith, *World War II Policy and Strategy: Selected Documents with Commentary*, Clio Books, 1979.

B Declaration of war on the USA and the British Empire by the Japanese Emperor, 8 December 1941

The 'Chungking regime' was the government of China.

More than four years have passed since China, failing to comprehend the true intentions of Our Empire, and recklessly courting trouble, disturbed the peace of east Asia and compelled Our Empire to take up arms. . . .

Eager for realization of their **inordinate** ambition to dominate the Orient, both America and Britain, giving support to the Chungking regime, have aggravated the disturbances in east Asia. Moreover, these two Powers, inducing other countries to follow suit, increased military preparations on all sides of Our Empire to challenge us. They have obstructed by every means our peaceful commerce, and finally resorted to a direct **severance** of economic relations, menacing gravely the existence of Our Empire.

Quoted in I. Nish, *Japanese Foreign Policy, 1869–1942*, Routledge & Kegan Paul, 1977.

C Staff discussions at Casablanca

Minutes of the Combined Chiefs of Staff Meeting, 14 January 1943. At the Casablanca meeting Roosevelt and Churchill made agreements about basic policies for fighting the war.

General George Marshall was the US Army Chief of Staff.

General Marshall stated that the peace of mind of the United States Chiefs of Staff was greater now than it had been a year ago. The Japanese are now on the defensive and must be careful of a surprise move from us. However, he pointed out that we must still worry about the locations of the Japanese aircraft carriers because they constitute a constant threat against our line of communications and for raiding purposes against our west coast.

We must not allow the Japanese any pause. They fight with no idea of surrendering and they will continue to be aggressive until **attrition** has defeated them.

Quoted in Jacobsen and Smith, *World War II Policy and Strategy*.

D Building the Kwai railway

The Japanese used prisoners of war to build the Kwai railway on the border between Burma and Thailand. The sufferings of the prisoners became notorious. This extract gives the views of one survivor, Major Basil Peacock.

The 'Geneva Convention' is a set of rules of war drawn up in 1864 and signed by many countries.

Men died of starvation, from the climate, exhaustion, accident, disease, and despair, and occasionally from personal assault. Diseases included dysentery, malarial fevers of all types, beri-beri, general toxaemia, sleeping sickness, jungle ulcers, and hook-worm. But the main killer was cholera. . . .

After more than three years on the Kwai, and discussion with ex-prisoners, I have come to the conclusion that the grim conditions were not due to calculated cruelty except in certain incidents. No nation at war uses its most intelligent and best troops to guard prisoners, so most of the Japanese personnel were substandard and some **mentally negligible**. . . .

Though Japan had not signed the parts of the Geneva Convention applicable to prisoners-of-war, the Imperial Government announced that it would conform to them. However, except in matters of pay and, oddly enough, permission to hold entertainments, they only carried out those which were convenient. The Japanese disdain for prisoners-of-war, especially officer prisoners, was very real, and it must be recognised that their soldiers were rarely captured unless too bemused by wounds or sickness to use their weapons. . . .

Every survivor [of the surrender at Singapore] knows himself to be lucky

not to be lying with 12,493 of his fellow captives (one third of the force)
in the War Cemeteries in Burma or on the banks of that beautiful and sad
Kwai river.

Quoted in *The Humanities Curriculum Project*, Schools Council/Heinemann, Sheet 662.

E The Japanese defence of Iwo Jima

A former US marine
describes how the
Japanese prepared for
the attack on this Pacific
island which the
Americans captured in
March 1945.
   'Banzai charges' were
infantry attacks with
swords and bayonets.
'B-24s' were long-range
US bombers.

The defenders' CO, Tadamichi Kuribayashi . . . had been among the first
to conclude that banzai charges, once so effective in Japan's earlier wars
with Russia and China, were futile against American firepower. Tokyo had
warned him that he could expect no reinforcements. He replied that he
didn't need them; the air attacks on Iwo had tipped off the coming
invasion, and transports had beefed up his garrison to twenty-one thousand
men, led by Japanese Marines. Kuribayashi turned his men into super-
moles, excavating the hard *konhake* [volcanic] rock. They built 750 major
defence installations sheltering guns, and blockhouses with five-foot
concrete walls, strengthened, in some instances, with fifty feet of earthen
cover overhead. Once he learned of the force about to attack him, Kuribayashi had no illusion about his future. He wrote to his wife: 'Do not plan
for my return.'
   Yet [they] were burrowing in. They meant to make the conquest of Iwo
so costly that the Americans would recoil from the thought of invading their
homeland. They knew the island could be taken only by infantrymen; the
US warships' 21,926 shells and the six weeks of B-24 bombing didn't touch
them; it merely rearranged the volcanic ash overhead and gave the invaders
dangerous illusions of easy pickings.

William Manchester, *Goodbye, Darkness*, Michael Joseph, 1981.

F A jungle patrol on a Pacific island

The description comes
from one of the most
famous novels written
about the Second World
War.
   'Recon' is an
abbreviation for
reconnaissance patrol.
   The author served in
the US army in the
Philippines during the
war.

[Martinez's] ears were searching the jungle ahead of him for some noise that
might indicate that men were waiting in the brush beside the trail; they
were also listening with disgust to the stumbling and muttering of the men
following behind him. . . .
   On the map there was only a half mile between 1st Battalion and A
Company, but the trail doubled and curved so often that it was actually a
mile. The men in recon were clumsy now and uncertain of their footing.
Their packs sagged, their rifles kept sliding off their shoulders. The trail
was crude; originally a game wallow, it had been partially enlarged, and in
places it was still narrow. A man could not walk without being scratched
by the branches on either side. The jungle was impenetrable at that point,
and it would have taken an hour to cut one's way a hundred feet off the
path. In the night it was impossible to see anything and the smell of the
wet foliage was choking. The men had to walk in single file, drawn up
close. Even at three feet they could not see one another, and they plodded
down the trail with each man grasping the shirt of the man before him.
Martinez could hear them and judge his distance accordingly, but the others

stumbled and collided with one another like children playing a game in the dark. They were bent over almost double, and the posture was cruel. . . .

At last [some men] would weave off the trail and go pitching into the bushes stupidly before regaining their balance. In the darkness such noises were terrifying. It made the men uncomfortably aware of how close they were to the fighting. A half mile away some rifles were firing.

'Goddammit,' one of them would whisper, 'can't you guys keep quiet?'

Norman Mailer, *The Naked and the Dead*, Allan Wingate, 1949.

G Kamikaze

Captain Inoguchi giving evidence during interrogation about the use of suicide fighters, 15 October 1945.

From October 1944 Japanese pilots volunteered to fly bomb-laden aeroplanes in to US warships. These pilots were called Kamikazes, literally 'divine wind' and also used to mean 'suicide pilot'.

'Bushido' is the Japanese feudal code of honour and chivalry.

At this time we in the PHILIPPINES thought about the approach of the crisis, owing to the odds. So we felt as follows: we must give our lives to the Emperor and Country, this is our inborn feeling. I am afraid you cannot understand it well, or you may call it desperate or foolish. We Japanese base our lives on obedience to Emperor and Country. On the other hand, we wish for the best place in death, according to Bushido. Kamikaze originates from these feelings.

It was the **incarnation** of these feelings. We believe in absolute obedience to the supreme authority who is unselfish, and whose concern is the welfare and peace of mankind. By this means we can accomplish peace. In view of this – from this standpoint, the Kamikaze deserved the consideration of the whole world.

The center of Kamikaze is morale. To achieve Kamikaze, the ordinary technique of the pilot is sufficient, no special training methods are necessary. Certain points about special attack are given. But to pilots who have had short training and least flight experience we give the essence of Kamikaze in the shortest period possible.

Quoted in Jacobsen and Smith, *World War II Policy and Strategy*.

H The war in Burma

A message from Churchill to Admiral Louis Mountbatten, 9 May 1945.

'Rangoon' is in the south of Burma.

I send you my most heartfelt congratulations upon the **culminating** victory at Rangoon of your Burma campaigns. . . . When these matters were considered at Quebec last September it was thought . . . that about six British and British-Indian divisions, together with much shipping and landing vessels, all of which, and more, were asked for by you, would be required for enterprises less far-reaching than those you and your gallant forces and Allies have in fact accomplished. The prolongation of the German war made it impossible to send the British and British-Indian divisions which you needed, and a good many other units on which you were counting had to be retained in the decisive European theatre. In spite of this **diminution** and disappointment you and your men have done all and more than your directive required. Pray convey to everyone under your command or associated with you the sense of admiration and gratitude felt by all at home at the splendid close of the Burma campaign.

Quoted in W. S. Churchill, *Triumph and Tragedy*, Cassell, 1954.

I   A British poster produced in 1945

ON TO JAPAN!

Glossary

attrition wearing down
culminating concluding
diminution reduction
incarnation embodiment, brought to life
infamy vile memory

inordinate excessive
mentally negligible below normal intelligence
severance ending
solicitation request

Questions

1   What do Sources A and B tell you about the causes of war? Explain why sources like these (a) are useful and (b) raise problems for the historian.

2   What evidence do Sources C and E provide about the difficulties facing the American commanders in the Pacific?

3   Read Source D and explain why, according to the writer, the Japanese treated prisoners-of-war badly.

4   From the evidence in Source E compile entries for an imaginary diary of a Japanese soldier preparing to defend Iwo Jima.

5   Source F is an extract from a work of fiction. How useful do you think it is as historical evidence of conditions for soldiers fighting in the Far East? Explain your reasons.

6   Using the evidence in Sources C, D, E and G explain the attitude of the Japanese to fighting and death.

7   From the evidence in Source H explain whether you think that Lord Mountbatten was a good commander.

8   What does Source I tell you about Britain's priorities in the Second World War? What other evidence of this policy can you find in this chapter?

Chapter 7 The Cold War: the Cuba Missile crisis

The Cuba Missile crisis was the most serious incident in the Cold War (a period of conflict, particularly between the USSR and the USA conducted by all means short of outright fighting between the two countries). Many people feared that a nuclear war might break out, and so it is important to ask whether the crisis was handled well by the American and Soviet leaders.

Introduction

The Americans often refer to Central America and the Caribbean as their 'backyard'. Ever since the early nineteenth century they have tried to prevent any parts of the region from coming under the control of an unfriendly government. In 1959 there was a revolution in the large West Indian island of Cuba and the new leader, Fidel Castro, became more and more friendly with the Soviet Union. The Americans were worried because, at its nearest point, Cuba is only 144 kilometres from the coast of Florida.

In April 1961 the US Central Intelligence Agency (CIA) helped some Cuban opponents of Castro to invade Cuba at a place called the Bay of Pigs. The operation was an utter fiasco and deeply embarrassed the new American President, John F. Kennedy.

At the same time the USA and the USSR were great rivals in the nuclear arms race. On 16 October 1962 intelligence officers showed Kennedy the first of a series of aerial photographs which revealed that Soviet missiles were being installed in Cuba.

A American options at the beginning of the crisis

President Kennedy's close friend and adviser, Theodore Sorensen, describes the options.
'George Ball' was Under-Secretary of State, that is, deputy foreign minister.

The bulk of our time Tuesday through Friday was spent in George Ball's conference room canvassing all the possible courses as the President had requested, and preparing the back-up material for them. . . . Initially the possibilities seemed to divide into six categories, some of which could be combined:

1 Do nothing.
2 Bring diplomatic pressures and warnings to bear upon the Soviets. Possible forms included an appeal to the UN or OAS [Organisation of American States] for an inspection team, or a direct approach to Khrushchev, possibly at a summit conference. The removal of our missile bases in Turkey in exchange for the removal of the Cuban missiles was also listed in our later discussions as a possibility which Khrushchev was likely to suggest if we didn't.
3 Undertake a secret approach to Castro, to use this means of splitting

him off from the Soviets, to warn him that the alternative was his island's downfall and that the Soviets were selling him out.

4 Initiate indirect military action by means of a blockade, possibly accompanied by increased aerial **surveillance** and warnings. Many types of blockades were considered.

5 Conduct an air strike – pinpointed against the missiles only or against other military targets, with or without advance warning. (Other military means of directly removing the missiles were raised – bombarding them with pellets that would cause their **malfunctioning** without **fatalities**, or suddenly landing paratroopers or guerrillas – but none of these was deemed feasible.)

6 Launch an invasion – or, as one chief advocate of this course put it: 'Go in there and take Cuba away from Castro.'

T.C. Sorensen, *Kennedy*, Hodder & Stoughton, 1965.

B An aerial photograph taken by an American aeroplane

The photograph shows the nuclear missile site in Cuba in October 1962. It was labelled by US intelligence officers.

C President Kennedy speaks to the nation

The speech was shown on television at 7.00 p.m., 22 October 1962.

Good evening, my fellow citizens:

This government, as promised, has maintained the closest surveillance of the Soviet military build-up on the island of Cuba. Within the past week, unmistakable evidence has established the fact that a series of offensive missile sites is now in preparation on that imprisoned island. The purpose of these bases can be none other than to provide a nuclear strike capability against the Western Hemisphere. . . .

This urgent transformation of Cuba into an important **strategic** base, by the presence of these large, long-range and clearly offensive weapons of sudden mass destruction, constitutes an explicit threat to the peace and security of all the Americas. . . .

But this secret, swift and extraordinary build-up of Communist missiles, in an area well known to have a special and historical relationship to the United States and the nations of the Western Hemisphere, in violation of Soviet assurances, and in defiance of American and hemispheric policy – this sudden, **clandestine** decision to station strategic weapons for the first time outside of Soviet soil, is a deliberately provocative and unjustified change in the **status quo** which cannot be accepted by this country, if our courage and commitments are ever to be trusted again by either friend or foe. . . .

We will not prematurely or unnecessarily risk the costs of world-wide nuclear war in which even the fruits of victory would be ashes in our mouth, but neither will we shrink from that risk at any time it must be faced.

Quoted in Sorensen, *Kennedy*.

D The odds on nuclear war

Theodore Sorensen describes President Kennedy's attitude to the crisis.

John Kennedy never lost sight of what war or surrender would do to the whole human race. His UN mission was preparing for a negotiated peace and his Joint Chiefs of Staff were preparing for war, and he intended to keep both on rein. He was determined, despite divided **counsel** and conflicting pressures, to take all necessary action and no unnecessary action. He could not afford to be hasty or hesitant, reckless or afraid. The odds that the Soviets would go all the way to war, he later said, seemed to him then 'somewhere between one out of three and even.'

Sorensen, *Kennedy*.

E President Kennedy's proclamation of the blockade of Cuba, 23 October 1962

'Sino-Soviet powers' are China, the USSR and their allies.

Whereas the peace of the world and the security of the United States and of all American states are endangered by reason of the establishment by the Sino-Soviet powers of an offensive military capability in Cuba, including bases for **ballistic missiles** with a potential range covering most of North and South America. . . .

Now, therefore, I, John F. Kennedy, President of the United States of America . . . do hereby proclaim that the forces under my command are ordered, beginning at 2 p.m. Greenwich time, 24 October 1962, to **interdict**, subject to the instructions herein contained, delivery of offensive weapons and associated material to Cuba. . . .

Any vessel or craft which may be proceeding towards Cuba may be intercepted and may be directed to identify itself, its cargo, equipment, and stores and its ports of call, to stop, to lie to, to submit to visit and search, or to proceed as directed. . . .

Quoted in R. Scheer and M. Zeitlin, *Cuba: An American Tragedy*, Grove Press, Penguin ed., 1964.

F A letter from Kennedy to Khrushchev, 27 October 1962

The first thing that needs to be done . . . is for work to cease on offensive missile bases in Cuba and for all weapons systems in Cuba capable of offensive use to be rendered **inoperable**, under effective United Nations arrangements.

As I read your letter, the key elements of your proposals – which seem generally acceptable as I understand them – are as follows:

1 You would agree to remove these weapons systems from Cuba under appropriate United Nations observation and supervision; and undertake, with suitable safeguards, to halt the further introduction of such weapons into Cuba.

2 We, on our part, would agree – upon the establishment of adequate arrangements through the United Nations to ensure the carrying out and continuation of these commitments – (a) to remove promptly the **quarantine** measures now in effect and (b) to give assurances against an invasion of Cuba.

Quoted in Sorensen, *Kennedy*.

G Views of the American press

(i) Private worries about Kennedy's action.
The 'alliance' is America's allies in the North Atlantic Treaty Organisation (NATO).

The political reaction within the nation and the alliance has been gratifying to the Administration, but it is misleading because it is not the same as private reaction.

Privately, there are several misgivings. First, many people find it hard to believe that the offensive Soviet missile sites in Cuba suddenly mushroomed over the weekend, and accordingly, there is considerable suspicion either that the official intelligence was not so good as maintained, or the Administration withheld the facts.

Secondly, many diplomats within the alliance still think it was wrong to confront Khrushchev publicly with the choice of fighting or withdrawing, especially since the security of many other unconsulted nations was involved. . . .

James Reston, *New York Times*, 26 October 1962.

(ii) Was the USA responsible?

'Some weeks before the Cuban confrontation, Washington decided that Khrushchev's cold war offensive, begun in 1957, was petering out. It therefore resolved on a showdown with Russia at a time and place of its own choosing. Khrushchev, with his Caribbean missile game, surprisingly also seemed to seek a test. He chose a time, October, that seems to have suited us.'

C. L. Sulzberger, *New York Times*, 25 February 1963.

H   Khrushchev speaking to the Supreme Soviet, 13 December 1962

The Soviet Premier is explaining the Cuba Missile crisis.

Our aim was only to defend Cuba. Everybody saw how the American **imperialists** were sharpening their knives and threatening Cuba with a massed attack. We could not remain impartial observers in face of this bandit-like policy which was contrary to all the standards governing relations between states and contrary to the United Nations Charter. We decided to extend a helping hand to Cuba. We saw a possibility of protecting the freedom-loving people of Cuba by installing rockets there so that the American imperialists, if they really decided to invade, would realize that the war which they threatened to start stood at their own borders, so that they would realize more realistically the dangers of thermo-nuclear war. . . .

Some people pretend that the rockets were supplied by us for an attack on the United States. This, of course, is not wise reasoning. Why should we station rockets in Cuba for this purpose, when we were and are able to strike from our own territory, possessing as we do the necessary number of intercontinental missiles of the required range and power? . . .

Only people who have taken leave of their senses can claim that the Soviet Union chose Cuba as a springboard for an invasion of the American continent – of the United States or countries of Latin America. If we wanted to start a war against the United States, we would not have agreed to dismantle the rockets installed in Cuba, which were ready for launching, for battle. We would have used them. But we did not do that, because we did not pursue such aims.

Thus, all the talk about Cuba being converted into a base for an attack on the United States of America is a vicious lie.

Quoted in H. Hanak, *Soviet Foreign Policy Since the Death of Stalin*, Routledge & Kegan Paul, 1972.

I   The seriousness of the crisis

The British philosopher Bertrand Russell exchanged telegrams with Kennedy and Khrushchev during the crisis. He urged them to avoid nuclear war at all costs.

'Florida' is the US state nearest to Cuba.

'Never before in the course of a long life have I experienced anything comparable to the tense anxiety of those crucial hours. I saw, in my mind's eye, the Russian ships sailing westward into the Caribbean and the US ships waiting to grapple with them. I saw, in imagination, the whole world in flames the next day, most human beings dead, and the survivors reduced to a condition of utter misery. Hour by hour, the desperate news was expected. Hour by hour headlines appeared in the Press such as those in the *Daily Sketch* of 25 October: "KHRUSHCHEV ORDERS SAIL ON – OR SINK. U.S. WAITS . . . WATCHES." Hour by hour, over wireless and television, came news of war preparations in Russia and even more frenzied preparations in America – warlike speeches by the President of the U.S. and other officials and the evacuation of the families of officers and troops in Florida. Hour by hour, nothing happened to stem the impending destruction of mankind.'

Bertrand Russell, *Unarmed Victory*, Penguin, 1963.

Glossary

ballistic missiles   rockets fired from the earth's surface to land back on the earth's surface
clandestine   secret
counsel   advice
fatalities   deaths
imperialists   people who take over control of other countries, especially for economic gain

inoperable   incapable of being used
interdict   prevent
malfunctioning   going wrong
quarantine   keeping isolated, i.e. the blockade of Cuba
status quo   established situation
strategic   for long-range warfare
surveillance   watching (here, by taking photographs)

Questions

1   Read Source A and explain why you think that options 1, 2, 3, 5 and 6 were not followed.

2   The photograph (Source B) was taken from a U-2 aircraft. From your own knowledge explain the importance of aerial photography in the Cold War (refer also to Chapter 3, Source A).

3   Why does Ted Sorensen in Source D say that Kennedy 'could not afford to be hasty or hesitant, reckless or afraid'?

4   Consider each of the following statements relating to Source E and explain why you agree or disagree with each.
   (i)   Kennedy claimed that the missiles in Cuba were a threat to the safety of the USA alone.
   (ii) Kennedy hinted that the threat from the missiles came not just from the Soviet Union.
   (iii) While the blockade was in operation no ships would be allowed into Cuban ports.

5   Source F contains the basis for a resolution of the crisis.
   (a) How much time had elapsed since Kennedy's announcement of the discovery of the missiles?
   (b) Make a list from other extracts in this chapter of the main actions taken by the American Government in the meantime.

6   Read Sources G(i) and (ii). In the light of these, how reliable do you consider Source C?

7   Compare Sources C and H. What do they tell you about the ways Kennedy and Khrushchev interpreted the crisis?

8   Read Source I.
   (a) In what ways are the views put forward here different from those in the other extracts?
   (b) How do you explain the differences?

Chapter 8 The Vietnam War: US involvement

The war fought by the Americans in Vietnam from 1965 to 1973 was the most bitter and controversial conflict in the world since the Second World War. Many people, including Americans, criticised the US Government for the war. But were these criticisms completely justified?

Introduction

For many years Vietnam, a small country in south-east Asia, was a French colony. During the 1930s and 1940s an increasing number of Vietnamese came to believe that their country should be independent. The leader of this movement was the Communist, Ho Chi Minh. During the Second World War Vietnam was occupied by the Japanese and when the French tried to take control again after the war fighting broke out between the French and the Vietnamese. In 1954, by an agreement made at a meeting in Geneva, the country was divided into two independent states. A Communist government, led by Ho Chi Minh, was set up in the north with its capital at Hanoi and a non-Communist government in the south with its capital at Saigon.

But the government of the Republic of Vietnam (South Vietnam) was cruel and inefficient. A Communist opposition army, called the Vietcong, was organised and fighting broke out. The Americans dislike Communism. Since about 1947 they have become worried whenever Communists have taken over the governments of various countries. In particular, by about 1960 the US Government feared that, if South Vietnam became Communist, other, neighbouring countries would 'fall' to Communism 'like a row of dominoes'.

Therefore, despite the fact that many South Vietnamese politicians were cruel and corrupt, the Americans sent help to Saigon. But as the war became increasingly fierce, so more and more American soldiers were sent; huge numbers of Vietnamese people were killed; and the rest of the world became increasingly critical of the USA.

A An Australian journalist's view of the government of South Vietnam

Ngo Dinh Diem was President of South Vietnam from 1955 to 1963.

Though there was no official censorship, the Vietnamese papers, knowing that their offices would be wrecked or closed down if they were critical, printed nothing that would offend the regime. Diem and many officials felt that the Western press should also serve as vehicles for his propaganda.

Considering the dismal situation of South Vietnam, Western reporting at this time was restrained. Television teams which came across examples of extreme brutality to prisoners refrained from shooting. . . .

The palace was filled with **functionaries** ready to carry Diem good news but singularly reluctant ever to pass on the bad. Diem talked but never listened; he looked but never saw. . . .

Diem was the victim of his family. They used, and abused, his position for their own power-seeking ends. The worst were Nhu and the little-known Can who ran Central Vietnam as his own **feudal fief**. Nhu was the most brilliant, the most irresponsible, and the most powerful. He ran South Vietnam like a gangland leader. His rackets included lotteries, opium, the Saigon water-front, extortion and 'protection' among Chinese business leaders, and **exchange manipulation**. . . .

Although [Nhu] and his wife were in many ways complementary. . . Madame Nhu seemed the stronger character. 'I shall never, never, never, never accept defeat,' she told me when she was working on her plans to crush the Buddhists. . . .

Sometimes she seemed at pains to make enemies and to shock. . . .

Her expression 'barbecued monk', which she used to describe one of the Buddhist bonzes who had burnt himself to death in protest against the regime's religious discrimination, is likely to stand alone for a long time.

D. Warner, *The Last Confucian*, Macmillan (USA), 1963, Penguin ed., 1964.

B   A letter from President Kennedy to President Diem, 14 December 1961

I have received your recent letter in which you described so **cogently** the dangerous condition caused by North Vietnam's efforts to take over your country. The situation in your **embattled** country is well known to me and to the American people. We have been deeply disturbed by the assault on your country. Our indignation has mounted as the deliberate savagery of the Communist programme of assassination, kidnapping and **wanton** violence became clear. . . .

They have thus violated the provisions of the Geneva Accords designed to ensure peace in Vietnam and to which they bound themselves in 1954.

At that time, the United States, although not a party to the Accords, declared that it 'would view any renewal of the aggression in violation of the agreements with grave concern and as seriously threatening international peace and security.' We continue to maintain that view.

In accordance with that declaration, and in response to your request, we are prepared to help the Republic of Vietnam to protect its people and to preserve its independence. We shall promptly increase our assistance to your defence effort. . . .

Quoted in USIS, *Why Vietnam?*, 1965.

C   Ho Chi Minh speaking to the National Assembly in Hanoi, 15 April 1965

'Napalm bombs' contain a substance which sticks wherever it splashes and burns fiercely.

Over the past ten years, the U.S. imperialists and their **henchmen** have carried out an extremely ruthless war and have caused much grief to our **compatriots** in South Viet-Nam. Over the past few months, they have frenziedly expanded the war to North Viet-Nam. In defiance of the 1954 Geneva Agreements and international law, they have sent hundreds of aircraft and dozens of warships to bomb and **strafe** North Viet-Nam repeatedly. Laying bare themselves their piratical face, the U.S. aggressors are blatantly encroaching upon our country. They hope that by resorting to the force of weapons they can compel our 30 million compatriots to become their slaves. But they are grossly mistaken. They will certainly meet with **ignominious** defeat.

Our Vietnamese people are a heroic people. Over the past ten years or more, our 14 million compatriots in the South have overcome all hardships, made every sacrifice and struggled very valiantly. Starting with their bare hands, they have seized guns from the enemy to fight against the enemy, have recorded victory after victory, and are launching a continual attack inflicting upon the U.S. aggressors and the traitors ever greater defeats and causing them to be bogged down more and more deeply. The greater their defeats, the more frantically they resort to the most cruel means, such as using napalm bombs and toxic gas to massacre our compatriots in the South. It is because they are bogged down in South Viet-Nam that they have furiously attacked North Viet-Nam.

Quoted in B. B. Fall (ed.), *Ho Chi Minh on Revolution: Selected Writings, 1920–66*, 1967, Praeger (USA), 1965, Signet Books ed., 1968.

D   US forces in Vietnam

These figures come from evidence by the US Department of Defense and the United Nations Secretary-General, U Thant.

Troops in Vietnam

	US	South Vietnam	NLF	North Vietnam
1961	3,164	338,000	63,400	•
1962	9,865	467,000	79,000	•
1963	16,500	525,000	91,700	•
1964	23,000	559,000	103,000	•
1965	181,000	679,000	230,000	•
1966	389,000	671,000	280,000	10,000
Early 1967	430,000	650,000	287,000	50,000

NLF: National Liberation Front – the opponents of the government in South Vietnam

E   The war through the eyes of a young US marine officer

Philip Caputo describes an episode shortly after arriving in Vietnam.

The wind kept blowing, relentless and numbing. Soaked through, I started to shiver. It was difficult to hold the handset steady, and I stammered when I called in the hourly situation report. I could not remember having been so cold. . . .

Around midnight, automatic-rifle fire spattered into one of the positions near the hamlet. The squad leader called me on the field phone and said that twenty rounds had been fired into his right **flank**, but without causing any casualties. There was another burst. . . .

Taking a rifleman along for security, I went down the road and through the village. Two M-79 grenades exploded in the tree line. The mud on the road was ankle deep. We could not see anything except a lamp burning in one of the huts. Staying close to the **culvert** at the roadside in case we had to take cover quickly, we reached the position that had taken the fire. There were a couple of bullet holes in the marines' **hooch**. It began to rain harder, although that did not seem possible. Huddling down next to the riflemen, I tried to see something in the black tree line a hundred yards across the rice paddies. The paddies had been turned into a miniature lake, and wind-driven waves lapped the dike in front of us. Then a white-orange light winked in the gloom. Bullets streamed past us with that vicious, sucking sound, and I went down on my belly in the mud. . . .

We slept fitfully for the rest of the night and woke up to a drizzling dawn. Dazed, the platoon hiked back to base camp, leaving one squad behind to guard the line. . . . Like prisoners in a labor gang, the marines marched toward camp joylessly and without expectation that the new day would bring anything different or better. Shivering myself warm, I felt more tired than I had ever felt before. I was worn out after only one night on the line, and I wondered how the platoon felt, after months on the line. I found out soon enough: they felt nothing, except occasional stabs of fear.

P. Caputo, *A Rumor of War*, Macmillan (USA), 1977, Arrow Books ed., 1978.

F American charitable work in Vietnam

Mary McCarthy, a distinguished American author, describes what she saw during a tour of South Vietnam.

A Marine general in charge of **logistics** in I-Corps district was deeply moved when he spoke of his Marines: moving in to help rebuild some refugee housing with scrap lumber and sheet tin (the normal materials were cardboard boxes and flattened beer cans); working in their off-hours to build desks for a school; giving their Christmas money for a new high school; planning a new market place. The Marine Corps had donated a children's hospital, and in that hospital, right up the road . . . was a little girl who had been wounded during a Marine assault. 'We're nursing her back to health,' he intoned – and paused, like a preacher accustomed, at this point, to hearing an 'Amen'); his PIO (Information Officer) nodded three times. In the hospital, I asked to see the little girl. 'Oh, she's gone home,' said the PIO. 'Nursed her back to health.' In reality the little girl was still there, but it was true, her wounds were nearly healed.

. . . There was only the one war casualty; the rest were suffering from malnutrition (the basic complaint everywhere), skin diseases, worms; one had a serious heart condition; two had been badly burned by a stove, and one, in the contagious section, had the plague.

Mary McCarthy, *Vietnam*, Weidenfeld & Nicolson, 1967.

G President Johnson addressing the Association of American Editorial Cartoonists, 13 May 1965

Lyndon B. Johnson was President of the USA from 1963 to 1968, the period when the USA's involvement in Vietnam was at its peak.

The war in Vietnam has many faces. . . .

The third face of war in Vietnam is, at once, the most tragic and most hopeful. It is the face of human need. It is the untended sick, the hungry family, and the illiterate child. It is men and women, many without shelter, with rags for clothing, struggling for survival in a very rich and a very fertile land.

It is the most important battle of all in which we are engaged. . . .

We began in 1954, when Vietnam became independent, before the war between the North and the South. Since that time we have spent more than $2 billion in economic help for the 16 million people of South Vietnam. And despite the ravages of war, we have made steady, continuing gains.

We have concentrated on food, and health, and education, and housing, and industry. . . .

Communist terrorists have made aid programmes that we administer a very special target of their attack. They fear them, because agricultural stations are being destroyed and medical centres are being burned. More than 100 Vietnamese malaria fighters are dead. Our own AID [Agency for International Development] officials have been wounded and kidnapped.

Quoted in USIS, *Why Vietnam?*

H   An interview with Ho Chi Minh

A British journalist, Felix Greene, interviewed the North Vietnamese leader for the *Vietnam Courier*, 16 December 1965.

Question: The United States began to bomb your country on August 5, 1964. According to the French Press Agency, from February 7, 1965, to the first half of November, 1965, there have been 17,400 raids by U.S. aircraft against targets in North Viet-Nam. We have been told that your communications and your productive capacity have been seriously damaged. However strenuously your people are resisting, how long can your country sustain this intensity of bombing without being forced to seek some way of ending the conflict?

Answer: As the saying goes, 'seeing is believing.' You have visited a number of areas in the North which have been savagely attacked by U.S. aircraft, you have seen the facts for yourself. So you may draw yourself the necessary conclusions.

In a war, there must be, of course, losses and sacrifices. Our people are determined to persevere in the fight, and to undergo sacrifices for ten or twenty years or a longer time, till final victory, because there is nothing more valuable than independence and freedom.

Quoted in Fall, *Ho Chi Minh on Revolution.*

I   A speech by U Thant, Secretary-General of the United Nations, 11 May 1967

The 'Democratic Republic of Vietnam' is North Vietnam. Hanoi, being the capital of North Vietnam, is therefore the government of North Vietnam.

Members of the Government of the Democratic Republic of Vietnam have repeated that if the bombardments were to cease there could be talks. It may be assumed that such a diplomatic stand has been taken by North Vietnam with the full knowledge of the position of its allies, and I regard this as a very important development.

The war in Vietnam has been divided into two phases: pre 7 February, 1965, and post 7 February, 1965. Hanoi showed a willingness to talk before that date (the date of the first bombing of North Vietnam) but has not shown such willingness since then. Therefore the first **prerequisite** to creating conditions for meaningful talks is the cessation of the bombing of North Vietnam.

Quoted in *Vietnam: Facts and Figures*, Friends' Peace and International Relations Committee, undated.

J An anti-American demonstration in London

It took place near the American Embassy, Grosvenor Square, 17 March 1968.

K Victory for the North Vietnamese

Philip Caputo describes the arrival of the North Vietnamese army.

The 'ARVN' was the Army of the Republic of Vietnam (South Vietnam).

The North Vietnamese Army simply rolled over the countryside, driving on Saigon. Except for a brief, hopeless stand made by a single division at the provincial capital of Xuan Loc, the ARVN offered no significant resistance. The South Vietnamese Army broke into pieces. It dissolved. There were terrible scenes of panicked soldiers beating and trampling civilians as they fled from the advancing enemy. . . . Not just an army, but an entire country was crumbling, collapsing before our eyes. The roads were jammed with refugees and routed soldiers. Some of the columns were twenty miles long, winding out of the hills and rubber plantations toward the flat marshlands around Saigon. They stretched along the roads for as far as we could see, processions that seemed to have no beginning and no end. . . . They were packed densely and stretched down the roads, solid, moving masses that rolled over barricades and flowed past the hulks of burned-out tanks, past the corpses and piece of corpses rotting in the fields at the roadsides.

Caputo, *A Rumor of War*.

Glossary

cogently forcefully
compatriots people of the same nationality
culvert ditch
embattled being attacked
exchange manipulation making money by altering the exchange rate of the country's money
feudal fief an area of land which, in medieval times, was ruled by an all-powerful lord

flank the side
functionaries officials
henchmen trusted supporters
hooch temporary shelter
ignominious humiliating
logistics organisation of supplies
prerequisite something which has to be done first
strafe attack from the air
wanton unnecessary

Questions

1 What evidence is there in Source A that the people of South Vietnam had a bad government?

2 What reasons does Kennedy give in Source B for sending military help to South Vietnam? Do you think any particular consideration weighed more heavily with him than any other? Explain the reasons for your answer.

3 Compare Sources C and G and explain how and why they differ in their accounts of the war.

4 Study Source D.
   (a) Between which two consecutive years did the US forces increase approximately eight-fold?
   (b) In what years was the South Vietnam army less than twice the size of the US forces in Vietnam?
   (c) How many more Communist troops were fighting in Vietnam in 1967 compared with 1961?
   (d) How many more anti-Communist troops were fighting in Vietnam in 1967 compared with 1961?

5 How useful and reliable do you think the evidence is in Source E and Source F? Explain the reasons for your answer.

6 Read Source G. Why do you think that Johnson says, 'It is the most important battle of all. . .'?

7 Read Sources H and I.
   (a) Calculate the approximate daily average number of air raids on North Vietnam from February to November 1965.
   (b) From the evidence in this extract and from your own knowledge explain how the North Vietnamese were able to continue fighting despite this American bombing campaign.
   (c) Why was the start of the American bombing of North Vietnam important?

8 Compare Source K and Source E. Both are by P. Caputo but an historian would consider Source E more reliable than Source K. Why?

9 Study Source J.
   (a) Were the protesters justified in holding a demonstration? Give the reasons for your answer.
   (b) Why was the demonstration held in London?

Chapter 9 The Arab–Israeli conflict: the Six-Day War

Of all the wars between Israel and her Arab neighbours, the Six-Day War was in many ways the most important and dramatic. It highlighted two questions, at least, namely: Who had more right on their side, Israel or the Arabs? What was the interest of the super powers in the quarrel?

Introduction

The state of Israel was created in 1948. Since then it has been involved in five wars with its Arab neighbours:
1 War of Independence, 1948–49
2 Suez War, 1956
3 Six-Day War, 1967
4 Yom Kippur War, 1973
5 Lebanon War, 1982.
The Six-Day War was particularly important for two reasons. In the first place, it showed the skill and determination of the Israeli armed forces compared with the Arabs. Israel defeated Egypt, Syria and Jordan in under a week. Secondly, as a result of these victories, Israel captured a huge amount of extra land.

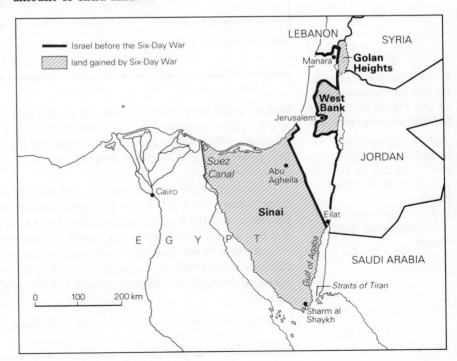

Why was it that Israel and her Arab neighbours were still quarrelling in 1967? The Arab countries had never accepted the creation of Israel (see Chapter 23); and so, Israel, a small country, was constantly frightened of being attacked, even destroyed, by these bigger neighbours. In particular, the country that was now Israel had previously been Palestine, a land mainly peopled by Arabs. The Palestinians, now angry and living in Egypt and Jordan, made raids into Israel. In fact, in the 1960s both Israel and her neighbours made frequent attacks across the frontiers. Finally, Israel had a particular quarrel with Egypt. From 1956 Egypt refused to allow Israeli ships through the Suez Canal. Then, in May 1967, Egypt also blockaded the Straits of Tiran to prevent Israel using her southern port of Eilat.

A   The Arab–Israeli joust

Daily Telegraph.

B   A statement issued by the El Fatah group of the Palestine Liberation Organisation

The statement was issued on 1 January 1965, the day of El Fatah's first raid into Israel.

The 'Assifa forces' were 'lightning' guerrilla troops.

Sixteen years have elapsed while our people live detached from their cause which has been shelved by the United Nations as a problem of displaced refugees, whereas the enemy plans with all his means, on the local and international levels, for an extended stay in our homeland, ignoring the heroic Palestinians.

In the light of this distressing fact, and because of the adverse effect of the lapse of time, the Assifa forces [of Fatah] have been launched to **reiterate** to the enemy and the world in general that this people [of Palestine] did not die, and that armed revolution is the road to return and victory. . . .

Regardless of sacrifice, our march will not come to a halt before the flag of Palestine is **brandished** once again in our dear homeland. We also vow to our people to continue on this path and not to **relinquish** our arms until victory is achieved.

Quoted in T. G. Fraser, *The Middle East 1914–1979*, Edward Arnold, 1980.

C The Israeli representative Gideon Raphael speaking at the UN Security Council, 24 May 1967

The 'Knesset' is the Israeli Parliament.

. . . it has been reported now from Cairo that Egypt has decided to initiate operational measures to interfere with the freedom of navigation in the international waterway, the Straits of Tiran. According to these reports, these measures include laying mines in the international waterway and opening fire on vessels which do not submit to search.

As the Prime Minister of Israel, Mr Eshkol, stated yesterday in the Knesset, interference with shipping to and from Israel, and the Israeli port of Eilat, would be an act of aggression. . . . The Prime Minister continued: 'From 1957 onwards other Governments, including the main maritime Powers publicly committed themselves to exercise their rights to freedom of navigation in the Straits of Tiran and the Gulf of Aqaba. Indeed what is now being challenged is a solemn and clear-cut international obligation. Its implementation will have a decisive bearing on international security and law. This is, therefore, a fateful hour, not only for Israel but for the whole world. . . .

The illegal proclamation by the President of the United Arab Republic [Egypt] to close the Straits of Tiran is another violation by Egypt of international law in addition to the long-standing illegal blockade of the Suez Canal which Egypt maintains in defiance of its international obligations and the resolution of the Security Council of 1 September 1951.

Quoted in Fraser, *The Middle East 1914–1979.*

D The start of the war in Sinai

This description is by Lieutenant Yael Dayan, daughter of Minister of Defence Moshe Dayan. During the Six-Day War Lieutenant Dayan had the task of supplying information to Israeli and foreign newspapers.

'Arik' is General Arik Sharon and 'Dov' is a colonel and, later, Yael's husband.

'Abu Agheila' was a heavily defended Egyptian town in north Sinai (see map). It is referred to later as 'Um Katef'.

Dov woke up, too late for breakfast and over tea told me that our big battle would be on Abu Agheila. He told me that it would be a tough objective, that in the Sinai campaign in 1956 we had made many mistakes in our attempts to take it. In 1956 our forces had not combined to direct a single blow but had operated separately, without recognizing sufficiently either the nature of the area or of the target. Arik, Dov and others had been with the paratroopers in the Sinai in 1956 and they projected a slight feeling of 'here we go again'. . . . Our main target was the defended locality held by the Egyptian 2nd division – Um Katef. The battle was planned for that night and during the day our forces were to approach it, destroying on the way several outposts and opening up the road to give our infantry a fast and easy approach. In 1956 those outposts had fallen relatively quickly and now we attacked them in several directions. . . .

I took off my helmet and listened to the radio. My father was talking to the soldiers. His voice was strong and clear – 'Soldiers of Israel . . . they are greater than us in numbers but we will hold them. We are a small nation but we are determined. We seek peace but we are ready to fight for our lives and our country. . . . On this day our hopes and our security are with you.'

Yael Dayan, *A Soldier's Diary: Sinai 1967*, 1967, Penguin, 1969.

E   The war in the air

Yael Dayan describes how the war in the air was won.

The 'West Bank' is the part of Jordan on the west bank of the River Jordan (see map).

The war in the air was won on the first day, 5 June. On that day the Israeli air force flew about 1,000 **sorties**. Over half the sorties were aimed at enemy aircraft on the ground, about one-quarter were directed against Egyptian ground forces in the Sinai and the rest were for transport interception and rescue.

On the first day practically all Arab air forces were wiped out. . . . Egypt lost most of its fighters and bombers in the first hour of the war. The Jordanian and Syrian air forces were attacked in the afternoon. Altogether, 452 Arab planes were destroyed. . . .

A total of 19 airfields were damaged in Egypt and 23 radar stations were destroyed. On the second day most sorties were dedicated to ground forces and interception. Air support was given to our forces in the Sinai and on the West Bank.

On the third day most of the sorties were for ground support. This continued throughout the fourth, fifth and sixth days of the war, supporting our forces in Syria, occasional interception, rescue, evacuation, etc.

Y. Dayan, *A Soldier's Diary*.

F   President Nasser of Egypt resigns

Gamal Abdel Nasser broadcasting the announcement of his resignation, 9 June 1967.

The 'United Nations Emergency Force' was posted on the Egyptian side of the Israeli frontier after the 1956 War. The 'Tripartite aggression' is a reference to three countries: Israel, Britain and France.

All of us know how the crisis started in the Middle East. At the beginning of last May there was an enemy plan for the invasion of Syria and the statements by his politicians and all his military leaders openly said so. There was plenty of evidence concerning the plan. Sources of our Syrian brothers were categorical on this and our own reliable information confirmed it. Add to this the fact that our friends in the Soviet Union warned the parliamentary delegation, which was on a visit to Moscow, at the beginning of last month, that there was a **premeditated** plan against Syria. We considered it our duty not to accept this silently. This was the duty of Arab brotherhood, it was also the duty of national security. Whoever starts with Syria will finish with Egypt.

Our armed forces moved to our frontiers with a competence which the enemy acknowledged even before our friends. Several steps followed. There was the withdrawal of the United Nations Emergency Force and the return of our forces to the Sharm al Shaykh post, the controlling point in the Straits of Tiran, which had been used by the Israeli enemy as one of the after-effects of the tripartite aggression against us in 1956. The enemy's flag passing in front of our forces was intolerable, apart from other reasons connected with the dearest aspirations of the Arab nation.

Quoted in W. Laqueur (ed.), *The Israeli-Arab Reader*, Weidenfeld & Nicolson, 1969.

G The Israeli view

The Israeli Foreign Minister, Abba Eban, speaking at the UN Special Assembly, 19 June 1967.

In three tense weeks between May 14 and June 5, Egypt, Syria and Jordan, assisted and incited by more distant Arab states, embarked on a policy of immediate and total aggression.

There was no convincing motive for the aggressive design which was now unfolded. Egyptian and Soviet sources had claimed that a concentrated Israeli invasion of Syria was expected during the second or third week in May. No claim could be more frivolous or far-fetched. It is true that Syria was sending terrorists into Israel to lay mines on public roads and, on one occasion, to bombard the Israeli settlement at Manara from the Lebanese border. . . . All that Syria had to do to ensure perfect tranquillity on her frontier with Israel was to discourage the terrorist war. Not only did she not discourage these actions – she encouraged them, she gave them every moral and practical support. But the picture of Israeli troop concentrations in strength for an invasion of Syria was a monstrous fiction. . . .

On May 14, Egyptian forces began to move into Sinai.

On May 16, the Egyptian Command ordered the United Nations Emergency Force to leave the border. The following morning the reason became clear. For on May 17, 1967, at 6 in the morning, Radio Cairo broadcast that Field-Marshal Amer had issued alert orders to the Egyptian armed forces. . . .

On the fateful morning of June 5, when Egyptian forces moved by air and land against Israel's western coast and southern territory, our country's choice was plain. The choice was to live or perish, to defend the national existence or to forfeit it for all time.

Quoted in Laqueur, *The Israeli-Arab Reader*.

H The view of the Eastern bloc

A statement by the Communist parties and governments of the USSR and six other east European countries, on 9 June 1967.

[The parties and governments] studied the situation that has taken shape in the Near East as a result of Israel's aggression, which is the outcome of a conspiracy against the Arab countries by certain imperialist forces, above all the United States. . . .

Struggling against imperialism for their freedom and independence, for the **integrity of their territories**, for the **inalienable sovereign right** to decide for themselves all questions of their domestic life and foreign policy, the peoples of the Arab countries are upholding a just cause. . . .

At a difficult hour for the states of the Arab East, the socialist countries declare that they are in full and complete solidarity with their just struggle and will render them aid in repelling aggression and defending their national independence and territorial integrity.

Quoted in H. Hanak, *Soviet Foreign Policy Since the Death of Stalin*, Routledge & Kegan Paul, 1972.

I   The US view

A speech by President Johnson, 19 June 1967.

Now, finally, let me turn to the Middle East – and to the **tumultuous** events of the past months. Those events have proved the wisdom of five great principles of peace in the region.

The first and greatest principle is that every nation in the area has a fundamental right to live and to have this right respected by its neighbours.

This last month, I think, shows us another basic requirement for settlement. It is a human requirement: justice for the refugees.

A new conflict has brought new homelessness. . . .

A third lesson from this last month is that **maritime** rights must be respected. . . . If a single act of folly was more responsible for this explosion than any other, I think it was the **arbitrary** and dangerous announced decision that the Straits of Tiran would be closed. . . .

Fourth, this last conflict has demonstrated the danger of the Middle East arms race of the last 12 years. Here the responsibility must rest not only on those in the area but upon the larger states outside the area. . . .

Fifth, the crisis underlines the importance of respect for political independence and territorial integrity of all the states in the area. . . . What [the nations of the region] now need are recognized boundaries and other arrangements that will give them security against terror, destruction and war.

Quoted in Fraser, *The Middle East 1914–1979*.

J   UN Security Council Resolution 242 Concerning Principles for a Just and Lasting Peace in the Middle East, 22 November 1967

The Security Council
Expressing its continuing concern with the grave situation in the Middle East. . . .

1. *Affirms* that the fulfilment of Charter principles requires the establishment of a just and lasting peace in the Middle East which should include the application of both of the following principles:
(i) Withdrawal of Israel's armed forces from territories occupied in the recent conflict;
(ii) Termination of all claims or **states of belligerency** and respect for and acknowledgement of the sovereignty, territorial integrity and political independence of every State in the area and their right to live in peace within secure and recognized boundaries free from threats or acts of force;
2. *Affirms further* the necessity
(a) For guaranteeing freedom of navigation through international waterways in the area;
(b) For achieving a just settlement of the refugee problems;
(c) For guaranteeing the **territorial inviolability** and political independence of every State in the area, through measures including the establishment of **demilitarized zones**.

Quoted in E. Mendelsohn, *A Compassionate Peace*, Penguin, 1982.

Glossary

arbitrary without consultation
brandished waved about
demilitarized zone area of land where no armed forces are stationed
inalienable sovereign right political right which no one can legally take away
integrity of their territories no land shall be taken away

maritime of the seas and oceans
premeditated planned in advance
reiterate repeat the message
relinquish give up
sorties flights to bomb enemy centres
states of belligerency being at war
territorial inviolability land shall not be attacked or seized
tumultuous noisy, disorderly

Questions

1 Look at Source A.
  (a) Look at the knight on the left. Who is the knight and who is supporting him?
  (b) Look at the knight on the right. Who is the knight and who is supporting him?
  (c) What do you think the cartoon is trying to say?

2 Read Source B.
  (a) Explain briefly what the group is saying.
  (b) What is the attitude of the group? Use words and phrases from the source to illustrate your answer.

3 Read Source C and draw a sketch-map to illustrate the case being made by Mr Raphael.

4 Read Source D.
  (a) Explain the reference to 'the Sinai campaign in 1956'.
  (b) Explain how the Israeli forces took advantage of the lessons of 1956 in 1967.
  (c) How useful and reliable do you think this source is?

5 List the targets attacked by the Israeli air force on the first day of the Six-Day War as described in Source E and explain the importance of these attacks in helping towards the Israeli victory.

6 Compare Sources F and G. Write an imaginary dialogue between Nasser and Eban about who was to blame for the Six-Day War.

7 What clues are there in Source H that the statement was issued by communist governments?

8 Is Source I a completely unbiased analysis of the Middle East problem as it was in 1967? Explain the reasons for your answer.

9 Compare Sources I and J. In what ways are they similar and in what ways different?

Part 3   Communism, fascism and democracy

Chapter 10 The Russian Revolution: the Bolshevik seizure of power

Ever since 1917 historians and others have argued about the Russian Revolution. Was it a genuine uprising of a downtrodden people? Or was it a well-organised takeover by a small group of political activists?

Introduction

Throughout much of the nineteenth century there was discontent in Russia: the peasants and town-workers were poor; the Tsar ruled without a parliament; and the secret police, the Okhrana, arrested people who tried to protest. During the First World War both soldiers and civilians suffered dreadfully especially through lack of food. As a result, in March 1917 there was a revolution – the Tsar was overthrown and a young man called Alexander Kerensky became head of a Provisional Government. (It was called 'Provisional' because there were plans to create a completely new system of government eventually.)

However, some people thought that Kerensky and his supporters would not bring about enough changes. One such group was a Communist party called the Bolsheviks. Their leader was Vladimir Ilyich Lenin. In March 1917 Lenin was living in Switzerland, having been chased out of Russia by the Okhrana. When he heard of the revolution he returned and during the months of April to November, Lenin and his supporters discussed the possibility of another revolution to replace Kerensky's government.

It was finally decided to organise the forcible overthrow of the Provisional Government. In November 1917 the Bolsheviks seized control and Lenin became the head of a new Communist government. When he died there were two rivals to succeed him: Joseph Stalin and Leon Trotsky. Stalin won, forced Trotsky into exile, and eventually had him murdered in 1940. (*Note*: In 1917 Russia was still using a calendar which was about a fortnight behind the one used by the rest of Europe. This is why in some books the 1917 revolutions are said to have taken place in February and October, rather than March and November.)

A Lenin's character

(i) A speech by Lenin's widow, Krupskaya, at his funeral in 1924.

Comrades, in the course of these days when I have been standing by Vladimir Ilych's coffin, I have been in my mind over the whole of his life, and this is what I want to say to you. He loved with a deep love all the workers, all the oppressed. He himself never said this – nor did I; I should probably never have spoken about it at any less solemn moment.

Quoted in Edmund Wilson, *To the Finland Station: A Study in the Writing and Acting of History*, Secker & Warburg, 1941.

(ii) A comment by Maxim Gorky, the most famous writer of the period of the Russian Revolution. He was a friend of Lenin, though very critical of the bloodshed and violence of the Revolution.

I have never met in Russia, the country where the inevitability of suffering is preached as the general road to salvation, nor have I ever known of any man anywhere, who hated, despised and loathed all unhappiness, grief, and suffering so deeply and strongly as Lenin did. . . . He was particularly great, in my opinion, precisely because . . . of his burning faith that suffering was not an essential and unavoidable part of life, but an **abomination** that people ought and could sweep away.

Quoted in Wilson, *To the Finland Station*.

B Lenin accompanied by Leon Trotsky in military uniform

Lenin is addressing a crowd of Russian workers.

C Lenin's arrival at the Finland Station, 16 April 1917

Lenin arrived in Petrograd (now Leningrad) after journeying from Switzerland. His arrival is described here by Sukhanov, a member of a different party from Lenin, who was present at the reception.

The 'gloomy Chkheidze' was President of the Petrograd Soviet or Revolutionary Committee.

A thunderous *Marseillaise* boomed forth on the platform and shouts of welcome rang out. We stayed in the imperial waiting-rooms while the Bolshevik generals exchanged greetings. Then we heard them marching along the platform, under the triumphal arches, to the sound of the band, and between rows of welcoming troops and workers. The gloomy Chkheidze, and the rest of us after him, got up, went to the middle of the room and prepared for the meeting. And what a meeting it was, worthy of – more than my wretched pen.

[Lenin then made a short speech.]

'Dear comrades, soldiers, sailors and workers. I am happy to greet in your persons the victorious Russian revolution, and greet you as the vanguard of the world-wide proletarian army . . . the piratical imperialist war is the beginning of civil war throughout Europe . . . world-wide Socialism has already dawned . . . Germany is seething . . . any day now the whole of European capitalism may crash. The Russian revolution accomplished by you has prepared the way and opened a new epoch. Long live the world-wide Socialist revolution.'

N. N. Sukhanov, *The Russian Revolution 1917*, trans. J. Carmichael, OUP, 1935.

D Lenin's letter calling for an uprising

Lenin wrote this letter on the evening of 24 October (that is 6 November – see note above) 1917.

The 'Revolutionary Military Committee' was a Bolshevik group under the chairmanship of Trotsky set up to organise the overthrow of the Provisional Government.

Comrades.

I am writing these lines on the evening of the 24th. The situation is critical in the extreme. In fact it is now absolutely clear that to delay the uprising would be fatal.

With all my might I urge comrades to realise that everything now hangs by a thread; that we are confronted by problems which are not to be solved by conferences or **congresses** (even congresses of Soviets), but exclusively by peoples, by the masses, by the struggle of the armed people. . . .

We must at all costs, this very evening, this very night, arrest the government, having first disarmed the officer cadets (defeating them, if they resist), and so on.

We must not wait! We may lose, everything!. . .

All districts, all regiments, all forces must be mobilised at once and must immediately send their delegations to the Revolutionary Military Committee and to the Central Committee of the Bolsheviks with the insistent demand that under no circumstances should power be left in the hands of Kerensky and Co. until the 25th – not under any circumstances; the matter must be decided without fail this very evening, or this very night.

V. I. Lenin, *Collected Works*, vol. 26, quoted in R. W. Breach, *Documents and Descriptions: The World Since 1914*, OUP, 1966.

E An American eye-witness

John Reed, a famous left-wing reporter, was in Russia at the time of the Revolution. This is his account of events on 6 November 1917.

The 'Red Guard' were revolutionary fighters, mainly armed factory workers. 'Smolny' was the Educational Institute which became the revolutionary headquarters. The '*yunkers*' were army officer cadets who supported the Provisional Government which had its headquarters at the Winter Palace.

Towards 4 in the morning I met Zorin in the outer hall, a rifle slung from his shoulder.

'We're moving!' said he, calmly, but with satisfaction. 'We pinched the Assistant Minister of Justice and the Minister of Religions. They're down the cellar now. One regiment is on the march to capture the Telephone Exchange, another the Telegraph Agency, another the State Bank. The Red Guard is out. . . .'

On the steps of Smolny, in the chill dark, we first saw the Red Guard – a huddled group of boys in workmen's clothes, carrying guns with bayonets, talking nervously together.

Far over the still roofs westward came the sound of scattered rifle fire, where the *yunkers* were trying to open the bridges over the Neva, to prevent the factory workers and soldiers of the Viborg quarter from joining the Soviet forces in the centre of the city; and the Kronstadt sailors were closing them again. . . .

At 1 a.m. a detachment of soldiers and sailors from Smolny occupied the Telegraph Agency. At 1.35 the Post Office was occupied. Towards morning the Military Hotel was taken, and at 5 o'clock the Telephone Exchange. At dawn the State Bank was surrounded. And at 10 a.m. a cordon of troops was drawn about the Winter Palace.

John Reed, *Ten Days That Shook the World*, 1926, Penguin ed., 1966.

F The view of the Provisional Government

An appeal by Vice-Premier A.I. Konovalov who was in charge of the Provisional Government while the prime minister, Alexander Kerensky, was at Military Headquarters directing the war against Germany.

Citizens! Save the fatherland, the republic, and your freedom. Maniacs have raised a revolt against the only government power chosen by the people, the Provisional Government. . . .

Citizens, you must support the Provisional Government. You must strengthen its authority. You must oppose these maniacs, with whom are joined all the enemies of liberty and order, and the followers of the Tsarist regime, in order to wreck the Constituent Assembly, destroy the conquests of the Revolution, and the future of our dear fatherland. . . .

Quoted in Reed, *Ten Days That Shook the World.*

G The storming of the Winter Palace

John Reed's account of the storming of the headquarters of the Provisional Government, 17 November 1917.

We . . . set off in the direction of the Winter Palace.

Here it was absolutely dark, and nothing moved but pickets of soldiers and Red Guards grimly intent. In front of the Kazan Cathedral a three-inch field-gun lay in the middle of the street, slewed sideways from the recoil of its last shot over the roofs. Soldiers were standing in every doorway talking in loud tones and peering down towards the Police Bridge. I heard one voice saying: 'It is possible that we have done wrong. . . .' At the corners patrols stopped all passers-by – and the composition of these patrols was invariably a Red Guard. . . . The shooting had ceased.

Just as we came to the Morskaya somebody was shouting: 'The *yunkers* have sent word that they want us to go and get them out!' Voices began to give commands, and in the thick gloom we made out a dark mass moving forward, silent but for the shuffle of feet and the clinking of arms. We fell in with the first ranks.

Like a black river, filling all the street, without song or cheer we poured through the Red Arch, where the man just ahead of me said in a low voice: 'Look out, comrades! Don't trust them. They will fire, surely!' In the open we began to run, stooping low and bunching together, and jammed up suddenly behind the pedestal of the Alexander Column.

'How many of you did they kill?' I asked.

'I don't know. About ten. . . .'

After a few minutes huddling there, some hundreds of men, the Army seemed reassured and without any orders suddenly began again to flow forward. By this time, in the light that streamed out of all the Winter Palace windows, I could see that the first two or three hundred men were Red Guards, with only a few scattered soldiers. Over the barricade of fire-wood we clambered, and leaping down inside gave a triumphant shout as we stumbled on a heap of rifles thrown down by the *yunkers* who had stood there. On both sides of the main gateway the doors stood wide open, light streamed out, and from the huge pile came not the slightest sound.

Reed, *Ten Days That Shook the World.*

H Trotsky's role in the Revolution

(i) Trotsky's own view of the part he played in the 1917 Revolution.

The revolutionary point of view ... was called in the workers' districts 'the point of view of Lenin and Trotsky'. During the years of the civil war those two names were always spoken inseparably, as though they were one person. ... Participants and observers, friends and enemies, those near and those far away, have tied together the activities of Lenin and Trotsky in the October revolution with a [firm] knot. ...

Leon Trotsky, *The History of the Russian Revolution*, vol. 3, 1933, Sphere Books ed., 1967.

(ii) The official view in 1951 when Joseph Stalin was Soviet leader.

On October 10, 1917, the historic meeting of the Central Committee of the Party took place at which it was decided to launch the armed uprising within the next few days. ...

Although at this meeting Trotsky did not vote against the resolution directly, he moved an amendment which would have reduced the chances of the uprising to nought and rendered it **abortive**. He proposed that the uprising should not be started before the Second Congress of Soviets met, a proposal which meant delaying the uprising, divulging its date, and forewarning the Provisional Government. ...

At a meeting of the Petrograd Soviet, Trotsky in a fit of boasting blabbed to the enemy the date on which the Bolsheviks had planned to begin the armed uprising. In order not to allow Kerensky's government to frustrate the uprising, the Central Committee of the Party decided to start and carry it through before the appointed time.

History of the Communist Party of the Soviet Union (Bolsheviks), edited by a Commission of the Central Committee of the CPSU (B), Foreign Languages Publishing House, Moscow, 1951.

(iii) In Stalin's time official photographs of the Revolution were re-painted. Compare this photograph with Source B.

I The British view

Sir Robert Bruce Lockhart, a British diplomat, was vice-consul in Moscow at the time of the Revolution.

What is important to realise is that from the first the revolution was a revolution of the people. . . . the revolution was a revolution for land, bread and peace – but, above all, for peace. There was only one way to save Russia from going Bolshevik. That was to allow her to make peace. It was because he would not make peace that Kerensky went under. It was solely because he promised to stop the war that Lenin came to the top. . . . even if Kerensky had shot Lenin and Trotsky, some other anti-war leader would have taken their place and would have won through on his anti-war programme.

R. H. Bruce Lockhart, *Memoirs of a British Agent*, 1932, Penguin ed., 1950.

Glossary

abomination something disgusting
abortive unsuccessful
congresses meetings of representatives

Marseillaise French national anthem, written at the time of the French Revolution and afterwards thought of as a revolutionary song.

Questions

1 Read Source A carefully. Which personal characteristics do you think made Lenin a great revolutionary leader?
2 Read Source C. Using your own knowledge, explain how accurate was Lenin's assessment of the situation in Russia and the rest of Europe in April 1917.
3 Does the photograph (Source B) provide any support for the view that the Russian Revolution was an uprising of the people? Explain your answer.
4 What evidence is there in Source D that the Bolshevik Revolution was a take-over of the government by conspirators rather than a spontaneous uprising of discontented people? Is this evidence reliable? Give reasons for your answer.
5 Why was it so important for the revolutionary forces to capture the buildings listed in Source E?
6 How do you think the following people would have responded to Konovalov's appeal (Source F): (a) army officer; (b) banker; (c) factory worker? Explain your answers.
7 The official Soviet view of the storming of the Winter Palace is that it was a great heroic deed. What evidence is there in Source G that this version is a myth?
8 Compare Sources H(i) and (ii).
(a) List the differences in the two accounts.
(b) Explain the reasons for these differences.
9 Look carefully at the two photographs and explain the differences between them. What does the second photograph tell you about the official Soviet view of the Revolution during Stalin's time?
10 Two of the extracts in this section are by an American (E and G) and one is a British view (I).
(a) How reliable do you think these sources are?
(b) Is one more reliable than another? Give reasons for your answer.

Chapter 11 The USSR under Stalin: industrialisation

Millions of people suffered great hardship and many died because of Stalin's ruthless policy of industrialisation. Was the goal of creating a powerful industrial nation worth all this suffering?

Introduction

Few countries have ever industrialised as rapidly as the Soviet Union under Stalin. But at what cost? When Karl Marx wrote about his theory of Communism in the nineteenth century, he believed that the working-class Communist revolution would take place first of all in industrialised countries. In fact, the first Communist revolution occurred in Russia, which, at the time (1917), had much less industry than, for example, the USA or Britain.

In 1929 Stalin took control of the Soviet Union (as Russia was re-named after the Revolution). He decided to make a number of changes very quickly. In particular he wanted to make the Soviet Union one of the most advanced industrial countries in the world. To achieve this in a few years seemed an impossible task. In the first place, the majority of Russians were peasants with no experience of factory work or mining. Secondly, all the other major industrial countries disliked Communism, so they were unlikely to want to help Stalin.

But Stalin was a determined and ruthless man. He did not care if people suffered in the short term if this meant that eventually the Soviet Union would become a powerful country. So he set about developing Russian industry through a series of Five-Year Plans. To meet the production targets (or 'norms' as they were called) workers were encouraged and bullied in various ways. Millions of men and women were forced to contribute by the most brutal ways. Some of the richer peasants were forced to go to the industrial towns by having their lands confiscated. Other people were arrested and used as slave labour in camps in the arctic conditions of the frozen north.

A   Stalin sets the pace of change

Part of a speech Joseph Stalin made to Soviet businessmen in 1931.

It is sometimes asked whether it is not possible to slow the tempo a bit, to put a check on the movement. No, comrades, it is not possible! The tempo must not be reduced! On the contrary, we must increase it as much as is within our powers and possibilities. . . .

To slacken the tempo would mean falling behind. And those who fall behind get beaten. But we do not want to be beaten. No, we refuse to be beaten! . . .

Do you want our socialist fatherland to be beaten and to lose its independence? If you do not want this you must put an end to its backwardness in the shortest possible time and develop genuine Bolshevik tempo in building up its socialist system of economy. There is no other way. That is why Lenin said during the October Revolution: 'Either perish, or overtake and outstrip the advanced capitalist countries.'

We are fifty or a hundred years behind the advanced countries. We must make good this distance in ten years. Either we do it, or they crush us.

Quoted in M. McCauley, *Stalin and Stalinism*, Longman, 1983.

B The industrial needs of the Soviet Union after the Revolution

An extract from the Communist Party's official history, written during Stalin's lifetime.

The 'large-scale collective farms' were created by joining a number of small farms together. They were then controlled by the farm workers. The aim was to increase agricultural production.

It was necessary [after the Revolution] to build up a large number of *new* industries, industries which had not existed in tsarist Russia – new machinery, machine-tool, automobile, chemical, and iron and steel plants – to organize the production of engines and power equipment, and to increase the mining of ore and coal. This was essential for the victory of Socialism in the U.S.S.R.

It was necessary to create a new munitions industry, to erect new works for the production of artillery, shells, aircraft, tanks and machine guns. This was essential for the defence of the U.S.S.R., surrounded as it was by a capitalist world.

It was necessary to build tractor works and plants for the production of modern agricultural machinery, and to furnish agriculture with these machines, so as to enable millions of small individual peasant farms to pass to large-scale collective farming. This was essential for the victory of socialism in the countryside.

History of the Communist Party of the Soviet Union (Bolsheviks), edited by a Commission of the Central Committee of the CPSU(B), Foreign Languages Publishing House, Moscow, 1951.

C A British historian's view

Professor Bernard Pares wrote his book in 1940, having made annual visits to the USSR for many years.

The 'komsomol' was the League of Communist Youth.

The very shortage of Russian skill and experience opened a vast field for the Russian Komsomol. Generally, the Russian working man had proved physically incapable of the day's work of an ordinary American, and here he was ordered to get in front of America. A Russian engine-driver was physically incapable of constant and hurried traffic. Russian laziness – so far the most common feature of the Russian character – in the factories took the form of evasion of hard or prolonged work. From this came all sorts of so-called 'breaches' in the prescribed plan; and into these breaches would be thrown a mass of enthusiastic Kosomols in a kind of economic panic to clear up the mess – to cope with the stoppage of a coal mine, or to gather in a cotton crop that lay rotting in the fields. And this work was also a school of administrative problems; young persons found themselves in positions of high authority and responsibility, where quick decisions and quick action had to be taken. One of them told me with pride the ages and posts of his colleagues, mostly under thirty-five. In this great school, with its countless and far-reaching opportunities, was educated a whole new generation of vigorous young men.

Bernard Pares, *Russia*, Penguin, 1941.

D Blaming the 'wreckers'

An extract from the Communist Party's official history.

The 'Donetz Coal Basin' is in south-east Ukraine.

[In 1928] a large organization of wreckers, consisting of bourgeois experts, was discovered in the Shakhty district of the Donetz Coal Basin. The Shakhty wreckers were closely connected with the former mine owners – Russian and foreign capitalists – and with a foreign military espionage service. Their aim was to disrupt the development of Socialist industry and to facilitate the restoration of capitalism in the U.S.S.R. The wreckers had deliberately mismanaged the mines in order to reduce the output of coal, spoiled machinery and ventilation apparatus, caused roof-falls and explosions, and set fire to pits, plants and power stations. The wreckers had deliberately obstructed the improvement of the workers' conditions and had infringed the Soviet labour protection laws.

The wreckers were put on trial and met with their deserts.

The Central Committee of the Party directed all Party organizations to draw the necessary conclusions from the Shakhty case. Comrade Stalin declared that Bolshevik business executives must themselves become experts in the technique of production, so as no longer to be the dupes of the wreckers among the old bourgeois experts, and that the training of new technical personnel from the ranks of the working class must be accelerated.

History of the Communist Party of the Soviet Union (Bolsheviks).

E A campaign against 'slackers, doubters and ill-disposed persons'

This poster was produced in about 1930 to help the campaign. The list is for workers to enter the names of other workers considered to be 'slackers'.

F Stalin praises efficient workers

In 1935 the coal-miner Alexei Stakhanov devised a system for doubling coal output. In this speech in 1938 Stalin praises this kind of achievement.

We have before us people like Stakhanov. . . . We had no such people, or hardly any such people, some three years ago. . . . Look at our comrades, the Stakhanovites, more closely. What type of people are they? They are mostly young or middle-aged working men and women, people with culture and technical knowledge, who show examples of precision and accuracy in work, who are able to appreciate the time factor in work and who have learned to count not only minutes, but also seconds. . . . They are free of the conservatism and stagnation of certain engineers, technicians and business executives; they are marching boldly forward, smashing the antiquated technical standards and creating new and higher standards; they are introducing amendments into the designed capacities and economic plans drawn up by the leaders of industry; they often supplement and correct what the engineers and technicians have to say, they often teach them and impel them forward, for they are people who have completely mastered the technique of their job and who are able to squeeze out of technique the maximum that can be squeezed out of it.

Quoted in J. T. Murphy, *Stalin, 1879–1944*, John Lane/The Bodley Head, 1945.

G The increase in production

Planned and actual production for the first two Five-Year Plans.

	Production 1927–28	Target first Five-Year Plan 1932–3	Actual production 1932–3	Target second Five-Year Plan 1937	Actual production 1937
Electricity (billion kw hours)	5.05	17.0	13.4	38.0	36.2
Coal (million tonnes)	35.4	68.0	64.3	152.5	128.0
Oil (million tonnes)	11.7	19.0	21.4	46.8	28.5
Pig iron (million tonnes)	3.3	8.0	6.2	16.0	14.5
Steel (million tonnes)	4.0	8.3	5.9	17.0	17.7

Basil Kerblay, *Modern Soviet Society*, Methuen, 1983.
Tony Howarth, *Twentieth Century History*, Longman, 1979.

H The first Five-Year Plan

Stalin describes the achievements of the first Five-Year Plan, 1928–33.

What are the results of the five-year plan in four years . . .?
We did not have an iron and steel industry, the basis for the industrialization of the country. Now we have one.
We did not have a tractor industry. Now we have one.
We did not have a machine tool industry. Now we have one.
We did not have a big modern chemical industry. Now we have one.
We did not have a real and big industry for the production of modern agricultural machinery. Now we have one.
We did not have an aircraft industry. Now we have one.
In output of electric power we were last on the list. Now we rank among the first.
In output of oil products and coal we were last on the list. Now we rank among the first. . . .

It is true that we are 6 per cent short of fulfilling the total programme. . . . It is true that the output of goods for mass consumption was less than the amount required.

Quoted in F. W. Stacey, *Stalin and the Making of Modern Russia*, Edward Arnold, 1970.

I The second Five-Year Plan

Professor Pares (see Source C) describes the success of the second Five-Year Plan which concentrated on the provision of consumer goods.

This [the provision of consumer goods] could only be done when the main plant had been laid down; but once it was there, set going with all the force and purpose of a Socialist State, the actual goods came out at a tremendous pace. In 1931 there were hardly any cars; by 1935 I found the streets covered with them. Naturally and of set purpose, as compared with the past, a levelling down went with the levelling up. Good boots were rare, but the unshod now had mediocre footwear. So it seemed with other clothing. The magazines and stores . . . were crowded with customers.

Pares, *Russia*.

J A critic of the Five-Year Plans

Roy Medvedev was a Soviet historian and a leading critic of the Soviet Government. His book was smuggled out of the USSR and originally published in the USA.

The first batch of experimental synthetic rubber was produced in January, 1931. Immediately the construction of one or two large factories was proposed. All the leading engineers, including Academician S. V. Lebedev, whose process had been to produce the synthetic rubber, doubted the practicality of such a program. . . . The specialists were astonished to learn that the government had decided, on Stalin's proposal, to build *ten* big synthetic rubber factories during the first Five-Year Plan. . . . The search for construction sites and building materials began. Such resources as were available were now spread out over ten units. Finally, in 1932–33, starts were made on only three factories; the rest were not built either in the first or in the second Five-Year Plan.

There were many similar examples of Stalin's incompetence and **adventurism**, which greatly complicated the already complex job of industrialization. Stalin's poor leadership was one of the reasons that industrial development at the end of the twenties and the beginning of the thirties cost much more than it would have with more **rational** planning and leadership. And if the extreme exertions and sacrifices which the people made for the sake of industrialization are compared with the results, the conclusion cannot be avoided: the results would have been far greater without Stalin.

Roy Medvedev, *Let History Judge: The Origins and Consequences of Stalinism*, Macmillan, 1972.

K Hardships suffered by the people

The winter of 1934–1935 was frightful, despite the lessening of the famine towards the New Year, the abolition of bread-rationing and the revaluation of the rouble at the equivalent of a rouble of black bread. . . . My son and I rationed ourselves to the limit, so that all we fed on now was a little black bread and 'egg-soup' (which I made to last two days with some sorrel and just one egg. Fortunately we did have wood. Soon I began to suffer from boils. . . . An enormous **anthrax** tumour under my left breast laid me flat on my back, and I saw the abscess devouring me. . . . I left for the hospital lying in straw on a low sledge. . . .

I no longer know how many weeks I spent in the **'gangrenous'** department at Orenburg's surgical hospital, during the bitterest part of the winter. The hospital was run as efficiently as the general destitution permitted; what it treated primarily was poverty. It was filled with cases of sickness or accident casualties whose true sickness or accident lay in chronic under-nourishment aggravated by alcoholism. The worker who lived on sour-cabbage soup, without fat content, would acquire an abscess as a result of a simple bruise, the abscess would be followed by septic inflammation and this, since the hospital fed its inmates very poorly, would last indefinitely. Children were covered in cold sores; whole wards were full of peasants with frozen limbs; bellies empty, clothes worn and threadbare, they offered small resistance to the cold.

Victor Serge, *Memoirs of a Revolutionary, 1901–1941*, OUP, 1963.

L A labour camp

Mrs Ginzburg was falsely accused of plotting against the government and spent the years from 1937 to 1955 in various prisons and labour camps. This passage is about her existence at a camp in Kolyma in north-east Siberia.

'Kostik' was a prisoner appointed to oversee the work and 'Keysin' was the timber-procurement officer.

It was about two and a half miles to the **shanties** where we were to live. We trudged along in single file through the virgin forest covered deep in slushy April snow. After the first few steps our feet were soaked, and when the afternoon frost set in our **bast** sandals were frozen stiff and we could hardly walk for the pain in our frost-bitten feet. As soon as the guards had left us, to sit smoking round a bonfire, Kostik came along to give us some perfunctory instruction in the art of tree-felling.

'Ever taken a look at a tree? No? Lord, what a set of molly-coddles. Well, you see the way the snow piles up round the trunk? The first thing you've got to do is to stamp on it till it's firm. Like this.'

It was easy enough for him to do it in his strong felt boots with elegantly turned-down tops and his breeches hanging over them in **spiv** fashion. When Galya and I (we were to work together) tried to imitate his movements, our sandals filled with snow.

'Now make a dint with your axe on the near side – after that you can start sawing. But do you two ladies know how to handle a saw? Lord, what a pantomime!'

'Do you really think that Galya and I can fell a tree that size?'

From Keysin, who had not yet left the camp, came the curt reply:

'Not just one. Eight cubic metres a day. That's the norm for the two of you.'

And Kostik, who until then couldn't have cared less about the trees or about us, chimed in, in a revoltingly boot-licking tone:

'Yes, and you have three days to get your hand in. You'll get full rations for that long. Afterwards it will depend on how much timber you can produce. We can't have any parasites here.'

Evgenia Ginzburg, *Into the Whirlwind*, Collins/Harvill, 1967, Penguin ed. 1968.

Glossary

adventurism   ill-thought-out schemes
anthrax   seriously infected boil
bast   tree fibre
'gangrenous'   decaying flesh on the body, usually as a result of a wound. It is in inverted commas in the passage because the hospital itself cannot be gangrenous; the word is being used to describe the awfulness in the hospital
magazines   warehouses
rational   properly thought out
shanties   badly built wooden houses or shacks
spiv   flashy

Questions

1   Do you think the businessmen listening to Stalin in Source A liked what he was saying? Give reasons for your answer.

2   Read Source B. What evidence is there in the extract to show that it is from an official source? Does this mean that it is reliable?

3   Read Sources C and D carefully.
   (a) How do these sources differ in explaining why some of the USSR's industries failed?
   (b) Which source do you think is likely to be the more reliable? Give reasons for your choice.

4   Look at Sources E and J. What do they tell you about the reasons for the poor efficiency of Soviet industry at the time?

5   (a) Using Source B to help you, explain why the government issued the poster in Source E.
   (b) Do you think the poster would have helped to increase production?

6   Study the figures in Source G.
   (a) Which industries achieved the target of the first Five-Year Plan?
   (b) Which industries achieved the target of the second Five-Year Plan?
   (c) Which industry increased its production seven-fold from 1927 to 1937?
   (d) What does the information you now have tell you about the success or failure of the Five-Year Plans?

7   Read Sources H, I and J and decide, giving your reasons, which of the following statements you agree with.
   (i) The results of the first Five-Year Plan were not as good as they could have been.
   (ii) The ordinary people of the USSR benefited more from the second than the first Five-Year Plan.

8   Read Source K.
   (a) What reasons does the extract give for the patients being in the hospital?
   (b) If you had been living in these conditions, how far do you think you would have blamed Stalin's policies for your situation?

9   Read Source L and explain the meaning of the following words: *norm*, *boot-licking* and *parasites*.
   (a) What does each of these words tell you about life in a labour camp?
   (b) What do they tell you about the attitude of the writer towards her overseers?

10   Using all the extracts (a) make a list of all the advantages and achievements of the Five-Year Plans and then (b) make a list of all the disadvantages and hardships. Do you think rapid industrialisation was worth all the suffering?

Chapter 12 Communist China: the Long March

The Long March is remembered in China as a very important and heroic event. Why were so many people prepared to follow Mao Tse-tung on this dreadful journey?

Introduction

China is a very large country and has by far the biggest population of any country in the world: one fifth of all human beings are Chinese. It is therefore not surprising that it has often been a difficult country to govern. From 1912 to 1949 China was governed by a political party called the Kuomintang. Its leader from 1925 was Chiang Kai-shek. But during this time there was much misery: local warlords refused to obey the government and the peasants suffered from heavy taxes and starvation.

Some men who wanted to improve conditions created a Chinese Communist Party. However, when they tried to organise an uprising in Shanghai, they were easily defeated by Chiang's army. One of the Communists, Mao Tse-tung, therefore decided to rely instead on the peasants of the rural areas. He organised his own Communist state, or Soviet, in the southern provinces of Kiangsi and Hunan; and he recruited his own Red Army.

In 1934 Chiang set out to attack and destroy the Communists. Mao decided to escape and march northward with his army and followers (including a number of very brave women). Of the one hundred thousand people who started this 'Long March', only twenty thousand reached the end of the journey – they had covered nearly 10,000 kilometres in one year and three weeks.

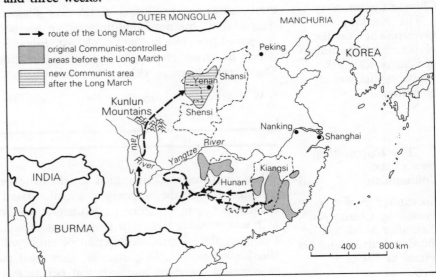

A Poem by Mao Tse-tung

This poem was written by Mao after crossing the Kunlun range of mountains. One peak, the Great Snow Mountain, reaches over 4,800 metres. Crossing it was one of the most dreadful experiences of the Long March.

Towering aloft
　above the earth,
Great Kunlun,
　you have witnessed
　all that was fairest
　in the human world.
As they fly across the sky
　the three million dragons
　of white jade
Freeze you with piercing cold.

In the days of summer
　your melting torrents
Fill streams and rivers
　till they overflow,
Changing men
　into fish and turtles.
What man can pass judgement
　on all the good and evil

You have done
　these thousand autumns?

But today
　I say to you, Kunlun,
You don't need your great height,
　you don't need all that snow!
If I could lean on the sky
　I would draw my sword
And cut you in three pieces.
One I would send to Europe,
One to America,
And one we would keep in China.
Thus would a great peace
　reign through the world,
For all the world
　would share your warmth and cold.

Mao Tse-tung, translated in J. Ch'ên, *Mao and the Chinese Revolution*, OUP, 1965.

B The problem of evidence

A British journalist who was on the staff of the *Manchester Guardian* at the time tells of the difficulties facing the historian who wants to find out about the Chinese Communists.

The 'Nanking Government' was the Nationalist Government of Chiang Kai-shek whose capital was at Nanking.

In writing about the Chinese Communists and the Red Army one is faced with many difficulties. Most reports of their activities have naturally been coloured by the prejudices of the Nanking Government and foreigners (mostly '**bourgeois**' foreigners) living in China. No impartial observer visited the Soviet areas in Kiangsi while the Communists were there and for that period one must judge almost entirely by what was found when they had left. Since their famous Long March to the North-west and, still more, since the beginning of the war against Japan when they became 'respectable', more reliable information has been available, but most of it is derived from one brilliant book, Mr. Edgar Snow's *Red Star Over China*, which he wrote after spending several months with the Communists in Shansi and Shensi in 1936.

J. M. D. Pringle, *China Struggles for Unity*, Penguin, 1939.

C The Kuomintang view of the Communists

An extract from a book written by Chiang Kai-shek after his defeat by the Communists and his retreat in 1949.

When the Chinese Communists sought to **foment** class struggle and instigate uprisings in the otherwise peaceful villages of China they found propaganda and agitation alone inadequate to achieve their purpose. They had to resort to such tactics of roving armed bands as robbery, kidnapping, killing of the victims, destruction of entire villages and the abduction of able-bodied people. In particular, they used the local **riffraff** and lawless elements to massacre landlords and rich farmers. They created a reign of terror among the masses and caused hatred between landlords and tenants.

Whenever the Communist troops entered a village or a rural town they would resort to burning, killing and **pillaging**, and set the people against one another. When they withdrew they would carry off all the able-bodied men in the area, leaving behind only the old and the infirm, women and children. Even the latter would be subject to the control and watch of the **Communist underground**. As a result they dared not talk to Government forces, much less to cooperate with them.

Chiang Kai-shek, *Soviet Russia in China*, Harrap, 1957.

D The rules of the Red Army

Edgar Snow, the first foreign journalist to know Mao Tse-tung well, describes the behaviour of the Red Army in the Kiangsi-Hunan Soviet.

The doors of peasant houses were hung on pegs and easily detached: they were sometimes used as beds with straw matting placed on the detached door as a mattress.

[The army] 'imposed three simple rules: prompt obedience to orders; no confiscations whatever from the poor peasantry; prompt delivery to the government, for disposal, of all goods confiscated from the landlords.' Eight other rules were adopted and put to music, to be sung and remembered by all troops:
1   Replace doors when you leave a house.
2   Return and roll up the straw matting.
3   Be courteous and polite to the people and help them.
4   Return all borrowed articles.
5   Replace all damaged articles.
6   Be honest in all transactions with the peasants.
7   Pay for all articles purchased.
8   Be sanitary; establish latrines at a safe distance from people's houses.

Edgar Snow, *The Other Side of the River: Red China Today*, Gollancz, 1963.

E Equipment for the Long March

The chief artillery engineer on the Long March talks to an American journalist who knew the Chinese Communists well in the 1930s.

Each man . . . carried five pounds of ration rice and each had a shoulder pole from which hung either two small boxes of ammunition or hand grenades, or big kerosene cans filled with our most essential machinery and tools. Each pack contained a blanket or quilt, one quilted winter uniform, and three pairs of strong cloth shoes with thick rope soles tipped and heeled with metal.

The people also gave us presents of dried vegetables, peppers, or such things. Each man had a drinking cup, a pair of chopsticks thrust into his **puttees**, and a needle and thread caught on the underside of the peak of his cap. All men wore big sun-rain hats made of two thin layers of bamboo with oiled paper between, and many had paper umbrellas stuck in their packs. Each man carried a rifle. . . .

Everyone going on the Long March was dressed and equipped the same. Everyone was armed.

Quoted in Agnes Smedley, *The Great Road*, Monthly Review Press, 1972.

F Crossing the Tatu River, May 1935

This was one of the most famous episodes of the Long March. The river is wide with a very fast current and therefore very difficult to cross. This is Colonel Yang Teh-chih's account of the crossing.

The eighteen heroes (the battalion commander himself included) were equipped each with a broad sword, a **tommy-gun**, a pistol, half a dozen grenades and some working tools. They were organized into two parties. The one led by Hsiung Shang-lin, commander of the 2nd Company, was to cross first.

The waters of the Tatu rushed and roared. I scanned the enemy on the opposite shore through my field-glasses. They seemed very quiet.

The solemn moment had come. Hsiung Shang-lin and his men – eight in all – jumped on to the boat.

'Comrades! The lives of the one hundred thousand Red Army men depend on you. Cross resolutely and wipe out the enemy!'

Amid cheering the boat left the south bank.

The enemy, obviously getting impatient, fired at the boat.

'Give it to them!'

Our artillery opened up. . . . Shells showered on the enemy fortifications; machine-gun fire swept the opposite shore. The boatmen dug their blades into the water with zest. . . .

The soldiers stood at the bow, ready to jump. . . .

I looked through my field-glasses and, just as I had expected, the enemy soldiers were **sallying out** from the hamlet. There were at least 200 of them against our few. Our crossing party would be fighting against overwhelming odds with the river at their back. My heart tightened. . . .

The two groups of landing heroes joined forces – eighteen of them – rushing towards the enemy, hurling their grenades, firing their tommy-guns and brandishing their swords. Utterly **routed**, the enemy ran desperately towards the rear of the hill. The north bank came under the complete control of our landing party. . . .

It was getting dark. More and more Red Army men crossed safely. Pursuing the enemy, we captured two more boats on the lower reaches which sped up our crossing. By the forenoon of the next day, the whole regiment was on the opposite bank.

Yang Teh-chih, 'Heroes of the Tatu River', quoted in Dick Wilson, *The Long March, 1935*, Penguin ed., 1977.

G A story from the Long March

Squad leader Hu Tung-sheng was in the habit of telling us the story about the cap.

He was a newly-enlisted fighter of sixteen during the Long March, with a peasant towel tied round his head. He had a great fancy for the regular cap worn by the older comrades, with its attractive **visor** and red star. He felt that, being a Red Army man, he was entitled to a cap! So he made a point of pestering the political instructor for one during the Long March. . . .

At this moment the political instructor came. . . .

It was obvious that, weak as he had always been, he was now at a very low ebb. But he always looked composed and never complained of being tired. He stopped beside Hu Tung-sheng.

'Oh, it's you! Why are you crying?'

'Political Instructor, I'm so hungry and I can't walk.'

Sitting down beside Hu, the political instructor massaged his leg. Then he fished out from his pocket the last piece of boiled ox-hide and offered it to Hu. At first Hu declined, being aware that the political instructor had had nothing himself for the past two days. But the political instructor insisted on his eating it and he was at last obliged to accept it. He felt a tremendous love surge through him.

Eating the ox-hide, Hu Tung-sheng listened to the political instructor. One must not sit here, the political instructor was saying: if he did, he would die. The revolution was hard, but it was for the happiness of all the Chinese people. . . .

Now Hu Tung-sheng felt warmer and strength came to him. The political instructor pulled him to his feet and helped him along.

Next day. . . Hu Tung-sheng was trudging along laboriously pulling out his legs, step by step, from the deep snow. . . . The political instructor had just fallen. He looked as white as the snow and was already at his last gasp. The political instructor recognized Hu and said brokenly:

'Never mind me . . . go on . . . don't fall out. . . .'

Hu Tung-sheng crouched silently in front of the political instructor. The latter took off his cap.

'Tung-sheng. . .' he said softly, 'the Red Army cap . . . take it. . . .'

Noticing the dilapidated shoes on Hu Tung-sheng's feet, he pointed to his own, still in fairly good condition, and said, panting:

'Shoes . . . mine . . . put them on . . . I am no more.'. . . When Hu Tung-sheng woke from his stupor, the political instructor's body was already cold and stiff. Only then did he realize the full significance of the political instructor's words: he must 'go on!'

Wang Teh-ching, 'The Red Army Man's Cap', quoted in Dick Wilson, *The Long March*, *1935*.

H Mao's view of the importance of the Long March

Speaking of the Long March, I should like to ask, 'what is its significance?' We say that the Long March is the first of its kind ever recorded in history. . . . For twelve months we were under daily **reconnaissance** and bombing from the air by scores of planes; we were circled, pursued, obstructed and intercepted on the ground by a big force of several hundred thousand men; we encountered untold difficulties and great obstacles on the way, but by keeping our two feet going we swept across a distance of more than 20,000 **li** through the length and breadth of eleven provinces. Well, has there ever been in history a long march like ours? No, never. The Long March is also a manifesto. It proclaims to the world that the Red Army is an army of heroes. . . . The Long March is also an agitation corps. It declares to the approximately two hundred million people of eleven provinces that only the road of the Red Army leads to their liberation. Without the Long March, how could the broad masses have known so quickly that there are such great ideas in the world as are upheld by the Red Army? The Long March is also a seeding-machine. It has sown many seeds in eleven provinces, which will sprout, grow leaves, blossom into flowers, bear fruit and yield a harvest in the future. To sum up, the Long March ended with our victory and the enemy's defeat.

Mao Tse-tung, *Selected Works*, vol. I, Lawrence & Wishart.

Glossary

'bourgeois'   middle class
Communist underground   secret members of the Communist Party
foment   stir up
li   about half a kilometre or one-third of a mile
pillaging   stealing with violence
puttees   lengths of material bound round the trousers from the knees to the ankles

reconnaissance   watch (on or by the enemy)
riffraff   rabble
routed   totally defeated
sallying out   rushing out
tommy-gun   light machine gun
visor   the peak of a cap

Questions

1   (a) Explain the meaning of Mao's poem (Source A) in your own words.
    (b) What does the poem tell you about the experiences of the Long March?
    (c) Why do you think he wrote the poem?

2   (a) Read Source B. Why do you think that it was so difficult to obtain reliable information about the Chinese Communists before 1936?
    (b) Look carefully at each of the Sources A to H and decide whether each one is reliable or not. For each source give reasons for your decision.

3   Compare Sources C and D. How do you explain the differences between them? Which do you think gives the more reliable view of the Red Army's behaviour. Explain your answer.

4   (a) Using Source E for your information draw a diagram with labels showing how the Chinese were dressed and equipped for the Long March.
    (b) Were they well equipped or badly equipped?

5   Do you think that Colonel Yang Teh-chih's account of the crossing of the Tatu River (Source F) is completely accurate? Give reasons for your judgement.

6   Using Sources F and G to help you, make a list of different personal qualities needed by the leaders of the Long March.

7   (a) Source G is a story of the Long March written in 1958. Why do you think the story was written so long after the event?
    (b) What message is the author of the story trying to convey?
    (c) How could you use this story as a piece of evidence about the Long March?

8   (a) Read Source H and using your own words make a list of all the reasons Mao gives for the importance of the Long March.
    (b) How far would you agree with Mao's views?

Chapter 13 Fascist Italy: Mussolini

From 1922 to 1943 Italy was governed by Benito Mussolini, whose character and ambitions had a great effect on the country. But did Italy suffer more than it benefited from his dictatorship?

Introduction

After the First World War there was much discontent in Italy. This was partly because many people were poor and partly because Italy was disappointed that it had not gained very much from the war. In 1919 Mussolini formed the Fascist Party – based upon the idea that the government should exercise strong power. This party gained many supporters because it claimed that it would make the government more efficient and the country as great as it had been in the time of the ancient Roman Empire.

Mussolini organised the Fascist Party, wrote about the theory of fascism and planned the take-over of the government in 1922. In that year Italy seemed to be on the brink of civil war. Mussolini gathered his Black Shirt supporters for what came to be called 'the March on Rome' and persuaded the king to appoint him as prime minister. Once he had become the head of the government he took complete control – he was a dictator known throughout Italy as *Il Duce*, the leader. He was also a great speaker and was able to rouse a crowd to enthusiasm when he addressed them.

A Mussolini's technique of public speaking

(i) The writer is Sir Ivone Kirkpatrick, who served as a diplomat in the British Embassy in Rome. He quotes Ugo Ojetti, who was a journalist with an Italian evening newspaper.

As an **orator** he was a master of every trick with which the **demagogue** binds his audience. His style, and he prided himself on the fact, was peculiar to himself and essentially un-Italian . . . his speeches . . . consisted mainly of short **staccato** sentences breathing self-assurance and conviction. But he could, when required, dramatize himself, using a **raucous** voice and ample gestures to pour scorn on his **adversaries** and to whip up the enthusiasm of the crowd. In 1921 Ugo Ojetti, writing in the *Corriere della Sera*, gave the following description of him speaking at the Fascist Congress in Rome:

'He is a most expert orator, master of himself, before his public always assumes the **mien** which best suits his subject and the moment. His gestures are sparse. He only **gesticulates** with the right hand. At times he puts both hands in his pockets. This is his statuesque moment in which, having drawn his threads together, he comes to an end. . . .'

Sir Ivone Kirkpatrick, *Mussolini: Study of a Demagogue*, Odhams, 1964.

(ii) Mussolini haranguing a crowd from the balcony of the Palazzo Venezia in Rome.

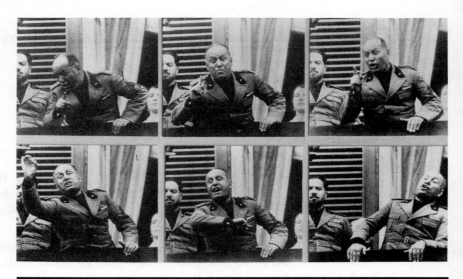

B How Mussolini came to power

This is oral evidence from an Italian lawyer who remembers how the Fascist Party gained supporters until they were ready to 'march on Rome'.

Neither I nor my most intimate friends ever bothered our heads about politics, we thought only of enjoying ourselves, but around us there was a political struggle, often real fighting in the streets between Fascists and anti-Fascists. At the time, many of the young Fascists were students and belonged to the middle and upper-middle classes; they were inflamed by the ideas of the extreme Nationalists . . . but mainly by the oratory of Mussolini, who, originally a socialist, had a kind of **mesmeric** personality.

During those years, almost every day one heard of the 'spedizioni punitive' (**punitive** expeditions), when the headquarters and clubs of the Socialists and Communists were attacked by the Fascists. During these spedizioni, the suspected Socialists, Communists or outspoken anti-Fascists were beaten up, or compelled to drink a large dose of castor oil.

Then in 1922, the march on Rome. We heard that the Fascist formations had converged from all the Italian provinces on the capital and they stopped at the outskirts of Rome. We heard that the King had refused to sign a document for the proclamation of a state of emergency and give the army the order to disperse the Fascist columns. Instead he had sent a telegram to Mussolini, asking him to Rome to form a new government.

Mussolini and Italy (from a recording), Longman, 1966.

C Mussolini makes a favourable impression on a British official

Duff Cooper served in the British Foreign Office, as an MP and held several Ministerial posts, including that of Secretary of State for War.

At Easter 1934 we paid a visit to Rome, where I had an interview with the Duce. I was favourably impressed. There were no **histrionics**, nor was I obliged, as I had been told would happen, to walk the length of a long room from the door to his desk. He met me at the door and accompanied me to it when I left. We agreed on the importance of rearmament and he laughed when I said that the idea that armaments produced war was as foolish as to think that umbrellas produced rain. Because he laughed at my joke I thought he had a sense of humour and was quite prepared to imagine he

'Ciano' was Mussolini's son-in-law who kept detailed diaries about events at that time.

had other good qualities. It is too early to pronounce a final verdict upon Mussolini. The more I read about him, especially in the pages of Ciano, the less I like him, but no trustworthy biography has yet been written, so that it is wiser to withhold judgement. He is not, like Hitler, condemned out of his own mouth, nor by the notoriety and magnitude of his evil deeds. It may be that he began well and meant well, like so many of the Caesars before him, but that he ended ill as they did owing to the corruption of power.

Duff Cooper, *Old Men Forget*, Hart-Davis, 1953.

D Mussolini's popularity

A British historian quotes from the autobiography of Mussolini's wife.

'Gargnano' was Mussolini's headquarters, 1943–45, after he had fallen from power.

In December 1944 Mussolini was raised to a pitch of exaltation which lasted for several days. He had gone to Milan . . . for a brief visit when abruptly, and for once spontaneously, his car was surrounded by a crowd of people cheering him as **vociferously** as if he had just announced that the war was over. Occasionally he was cheered at Gargnano, but he had never been received like this. The crowds increased as the car drove slowly through the streets, until even anti-Fascist observers had to admit that as many as 40,000 people were excitedly shouting, '*Duce! Duce! Duce!*' at the top of their voices. 'Had I not heard the frantic cheering on the radio,' Rachele [his wife] said, 'I could scarcely have believed Benito's account of his experiences when he got back. It simply cannot be true that the whole country is against Fascism, or that everyone hates him.'

'In twenty years of Fascism,' he told her proudly, 'I have never had such a welcome. . . . When I had finished speaking the ovation was thrilling – an absolute triumph. As for the crowds, they were like a tidal wave. It was wonderful to be among the people, standing up in the car and to hear their shouts of loyalty.'

Christopher Hibbert, *Benito Mussolini*, Longman, 1962.

E Mussolini's lack of ability as an administrator

During his diplomatic career Sir Ivone Kirkpatrick knew Mussolini and interviewed many former Fascist leaders after the Second World War.

Mussolini knew very little about the machinery of government or economics or foreign countries. His ignorance was sometimes staggering. . . . Figures meant little or nothing to him. One million was a large figure. So was ten millions or a hundred millions; and he found it difficult to distinguish between them. . . .

Having no stomach for the grind of administrative work, it was Mussolini's practice in the early days to leave to his ministers the management of their departments, reserving to himself only major decisions of policy and the right to intervene **capriciously** in details such as the determination of the date on which the Rome police changed into their white summer uniforms.

Kirkpatrick, *Mussolini: Study of a Demagogue*.

F Mussolini writing about fascism

This is an extract from Mussolini's article in the *Enciclopedia Italiana*.

Fascism rejects pacifism. Pacifism conceals an escape from struggle. Pacifism is cowardice in the face of sacrifice. War alone brings all human energy to its highest pitch and puts the stamp of nobility upon the peoples who have the courage to meet it. All other trials are substitutes which never really put men into the position in which they must must make the great decision – the alternative between life or death. Thus, any doctrine which is founded on the **postulate** of peace is hostile to Fascism.

'Fascism' in *Enciclopedia Italiana*.

G Mussolini's aims

The American Ambassador in Rome wrote this book on behalf of Mussolini from notes taken in interviews with him from 1921 to 1924.

My objective is simple; I want to make Italy great, respected, and feared; I want to **render** my Nation worthy of her noble and ancient traditions. I want to accelerate her **evolution** towards the highest forms of national co-operation, I want to make a greater prosperity always possible for the whole people. I want to create a political organization to express, to guarantee and to safeguard our development. I am tireless in my wish to see newly born and newly reborn Italians. With all my strength, with all my energies, without pause, without interruptions I want to bring them to their fullest opportunities. . . . I, like the most devoted of citizens, place upon myself and on every beat of my heart service to the Italian people. I proclaim myself their servant. I feel that all Italians understand and love me.

Benito Mussolini, *My Autobiography*, translated by R. W. Child, 1928, Paternoster Library ed., 1936.

H Mussolini's thoughts about war in 1939

Edda Mussolini Ciano writes about her father's views. She was married to the Italian Foreign Minister, Count Ciano.

[In the crisis leading to the Second World] he had never been against an armed conflict. On the contrary, he had two reasons for thinking it to be essential: 1) in his opinion, war strengthened the people of a nation; 2) a new victory by the Italian armed forces would give Italy the territories and respect that it had needed for many years, not so that it might enslave other peoples, but so that it would be convinced that it was no longer an under-developed country looked down upon throughout the world.

Edda Mussolini Ciano, as told to Albert Zarca, *My Truth*, Weidenfeld & Nicolson, 1976.

I The evil of fascism

Four Italians wrote this book under the pen-name of 'Pentad'. They were in exile in Britain at the time and did not dare reveal their true

[The journalists'] task was simply that of **perpetuating** the feeling of disorder and danger in Italy and in the world, so as to justify **implicitly** the tight **fetters** of Fascism about liberty and about the Italian people. It was necessary to convince the people that the 'genius' of the Duce was carrying out mysterious designs, of which he alone had the secret; that Italy was

names for fear that relations still living in Italy would be ill-treated because of their criticisms of Mussolini's government.

assailed and menaced by all the rest of the world, and that it was therefore necessary to remain constantly on a war footing. 'War' and 'genius' justify all crimes, even if these crimes are not only immoral, but absurd. . . . and it can be said that the Fascist regime itself has concentrated on only two problems: police and propaganda. . . .

Spied upon everywhere – in the office, in the factory, at work, inside and outside the home – Italians are subjected to a continual process of corruption and intimidation which the constant lowering in the standard of living and the increase in taxes of all kinds make more effective.

'Pentad', *The Remaking of Italy*, Penguin, 1941.

Glossary

adversaries opponents, enemies
assailed attacked
capriciously unpredictably
demagogue a political agitator who wins support by his public speaking
evolution gradual change
fetters chains fitted on prisoners
gesticulates makes expressive movements with the hands and arms
histrionics putting on an act
implicitly indirectly

mesmeric holding people spell-bound
mien manner
orator very good public speaker
perpetuating maintaining
postulate basis of an argument
punitive for punishment
raucous harsh, loud
render cause to be
staccato cut short
vociferously noisily

Questions

1 Study Sources A(i) and A(ii).
  (a) How do they show Mussolini's skill as an orator?
  (b) Why was this skill so important?
2 The speaker in Source B is recalling events over forty years after they occurred. Give reasons for and against his being a reliable source.
3 (a) In Source C was the writer's view of Mussolini changed by the meeting? Give details.
  (b) Why does the writer think that it is significant that Mussolini laughed when he said: 'the idea that armaments produced war was as foolish as to think that umbrellas produced rain'?
4 Study Source D.
  (a) Using your own knowledge also, say why Mussolini 'was raised to a pitch of exaltation'.
  (b) Was he surprised by this reception? Give reasons for your answer.
5 Look at Sources E and G.
  (a) In what ways do the two views conflict?
  (b) How reliable do you think the two sources are as evidence?
6 (a) What evidence is there in Sources F and H that Mussolini loved violence and war?
  (b) According to these sources, what was fascism doing for Italy?
7 Read Source I. Do you think that the authors were right to believe that Mussolini would object to their book? Explain the reasons for your answer.
8 From the evidence in this chapter how far do you think that Mussolini was a popular leader?
9 Using the evidence in this chapter describe Mussolini's methods of converting Italy into a fascist state.

Chapter 14 The USA: the New Deal

President Franklin Roosevelt came to power in 1933 determined to solve the economic crisis in the USA. People have sharply disagreed about the way he tackled the crisis – both at the time and since. Did he use the right policies? Were there alternatives?

Introduction

For many Americans the 1920s were the years of gaiety and wealth. Many rich people obtained their money by buying stocks and shares, which increased in value. Then suddenly in 1929 came the 'Great Crash': the value of stocks and shares tumbled; banks had to close; and many businessmen were financially ruined. As businesses closed down the unemployment figures steadily rose. Poverty and misery spread. People had to leave their homes because they could not pay the mortgages; queues stretched along pavements as men lined up for relief money; other people clustered round free 'soup kitchens' to avoid starvation. The government seemed unable or unwilling to cope.

In the run-up to the Presidential election of November 1932 the Democratic Party chose as their candidate the Governor of New York, Franklin Roosevelt. In his speech accepting the nomination as candidate he declared, 'I pledge you, I pledge myself to a new deal for the American people.'

Roosevelt won the election and plunged with great energy and speed into passing laws and providing government money to cope with unemployment. Roosevelt was President from 1933 until his death in 1945 and until the outbreak of the Second World War he devoted himself to his country's economic recovery.

A The origin of the term 'New Deal'

Dorothy, the wife of Sam Rosenman who was a close friend of Roosevelt, describes how her husband introduced the term.

Sam coined the term 'New Deal'. On that night in 1932 when it didn't look as though Roosevelt was going to be nominated, Sam went into another room and wrote a **peroration** he hoped Roosevelt was going to be able to deliver. He used the term, 'the New Deal'. The cartoonist Roland Kirby picked up that phrase, and the next day there was a picture of a plane flying from Albany to Chicago and on its wings were **emblazoned** 'The New Deal.'

Quoted in K. Louchheim (ed.), *The Making of the New Deal: the Insiders Speak*, Harvard University Press, 1983.

B Roosevelt's inaugural address as President

In his inaugural address (that is, his first introductory speech as President) of 4 March 1933, Roosevelt describes the problems facing many American citizens.

. . . let me assert my firm belief that the only thing we have to fear is fear itself – nameless, unreasoning, unjustified terror which paralyzes needed efforts to convert retreat into advance. . . . Values have shrunken to fantastic levels; taxes have risen; our ability to pay has fallen, government of all kinds is faced by serious **curtailment** of income; the means of exchange are frozen in the currents of trade; the withered leaves of industrial enterprise lie on every side; farmers find no markets for their produce; the savings of many years in thousands of families are gone.

More important, a host of unemployed citizens face the grim problem of existence, and an equally great number toil with little return. Only a foolish optimist can deny the dark realities of the moment.

Yet our distress comes from no failure of substance. We are stricken by no plague of locusts. Compared with the perils which our forefathers conquered because they believed and were not afraid, we still have much to be thankful for. Nature still offers her bounty, and human efforts have multiplied it. Plenty is at our doorstep, but a generous use of it languishes in the very sight of the supply.

Quoted in J. Chandler, *Life, Liberty and the Pursuit of Happiness*, OUP, 1971.

C Roosevelt's speech on signing the National Recovery Act, 1933

This was one of the key measures in the New Deal in its attempt to reduce the level of unemployment.

The law I have just signed was passed to *put people back to work*, to let them buy more of the products of farms and factories and start our business at a living rate again. This task is in two stages; first, to get many hundreds of thousands of the unemployed back on the payroll by snowfall and, second, to plan for a better future for the longer pull. While we shall not neglect the second, the first stage is an emergency job. It has the right of way.

The second part of the Act gives employment through a vast program of public works. Our studies show that we should be able to hire many men at once and to step up to about a million new jobs by 1 October, and a much greater number later. We must put at the head of our list those works which are fully ready to start now. Our first purpose is to create employment as fast as we can, but we should not pour money into unproved projects. . . .

In my Inaugural I laid down the simple proposition that nobody is going to starve in this country. It seems to me to be equally plain that no business which depends for its existence on paying less than living wages to its workers has any right to continue in this country.

Quoted in Chandler, *Life, Liberty and the Pursuit of Happiness*.

D   Roosevelt in a hurry

This cartoon appeared in the *Kansas City Star* in 1933.

E   The work of the Tennessee Valley Authority (TVA)

The most ambitious of the New Deal schemes. The area involved several states. Here its work is described by the TVA's director.

This is an entirely different region from what it was ten years ago. . . .

You can see the change best of all if you have flown down the valley from time to time, as I have done so frequently during these past ten years. . . . You can see the undulation of neatly terraced hillsides, newly contrived to make the beating rains 'walk, not run, to the nearest exit'; you can see the grey bulk of the dams, stout marks across the river now deep blue, no longer red and murky with its hoard of soil washed from the eroding land. You can see the barges with their double tows of goods to be unloaded at new river terminals. And marching towards every point on the horizon you can see the steel criss-cross of electric transmission towers, a twentieth-century tower standing in a cover beside an eighteenth-century mountain cabin, a symbol and a summary of the change. . . .

The **jurisdiction** of the TVA cut across existing lines of federal bureaus and departments. A single agency, instead of half a dozen, was to design and build the dams, buy the land, construct transmission lines, and market the power the river produced. . . . The contrast between such an administrative scheme for the Tennessee River and the plans on other rivers is illustrated by a contrasting instance, where one set of men designed a dam, another agency actually built it, a third group of men then took over the operation and maintenance of one part of the dam, still a fourth group another part, a fifth disposes of one share of the output – each acting under separate direction and policies, with the power of decision for the several parts of the task centered in different hands in distant places.

David Lilienthal, *TVA: Tennessee Valley Authority – Democracy on the March*, Penguin, 1944.

F Part of the TVA Ballad

A popular song at the time of the New Deal.

My name is William Edwards, I live down Cove Creek way,
I'm working on a project they call the T.V.A.

The government began it when I was but a child,
But now they are in earnest and Tennessee's gone wild.

Oh, see them boys a-comin' – their government they trust;
Just hear their hammers ringin' – they'll build that dam or bust.

I meant to marry Sally, but work I could not find;
The T.V.A. was started and surely eased my mind.

I'm writing her a letter, these words I'll surely say:
'The Government has saved us, just name our wedding day.'

Oh, things looked blue and lonely until this come along;
Now hear the crew a-singing' and listen to their song.

'The Government employs us, short hours and certain pay;
Oh, things are up and comin', God bless the T.V.A.'

O. Downes and E. Siegmeister, *A Treasury of American Song*, Consolidated Music Publishers Inc., 1943.

G An imaginary conversation

This satirical piece was published in 1938, during Roosevelt's second term of office.
The 'W.P.A.' was the Works Projects Administration – a scheme for giving work to the unemployed.

Q: What about the WPA, Mr. Arbuthnot?
A: Oh, the shovel brigade. I'm against the WPA and the PWA and all this alphabet-soup stuff. Say, speaking of the WPA, did you hear the one about the WPA worker and King Solomon? Why is a WPA worker like King Solomon?
Q: I heard it. Now then –
A: Because he takes his pick and goes to bed.
Q: Is that the funniest New Deal joke you know, Mr. Arbuthnot?
A: Oh, no. Here's the funniest. Have you heard there's only Six Dwarfs now?
Q: Only six?
A: Yeah. Dopey's in the White House.
Q: Mr. Arbuthnot, you slay me. Well, go on. Tell us more. Why don't you like Mr. Roosevelt? What's the matter with him?
A: Well, the trouble with Roosevelt is he's an idealist.
Q: Yes?
A: And the trouble with Roosevelt is he's destroyed individual initiative.
Q: Do tell.
A: And the trouble with Roosevelt is he's a Communist.
Q: I see. Go on.
A: The trouble with Roosevelt is he's a Fascist.
Q: A Fascist too?
A: Certainly. He wants to be a dictator. Don't tell *me* he hasn't got his eye on a third term.
Q: Snakes alive! Has he?

A: And the trouble with Roosevelt is his vanity. That's what makes him so stubborn. He just won't listen to reason. And the trouble with Roosevelt is he's got no right to spend the taxpayers' money to build up his own personal political machine.

Frank Sullivan, 'The Cliché Expert Testifies as a Roosevelt Hater' in *A Pearl in Every Oyster*, 1938, quoted in W. E. Leuchtenburg, *The New Deal: A Documentary History*, Harper & Row, 1968.

H   Unemployment in the USA as a percentage of the total labour force

1923	1930	1931	1932	1933	1934	1935	1936	1937	1938
3.2	8.7	15.8	23.6	24.9	26.7	20.1	16.9	14.3	19.0

I   Roosevelt – dictator, revolutionary or failure?

(i) The British politician Winston Churchill discusses the accusation made by some people that Roosevelt was behaving like a dictator.

[Roosevelt] arrived at the summit of the greatest economic community in the world at the moment of its extreme embarrassment. Everybody had lost faith in everything. . . . We must never forget that this was the basis from which he started. Supreme power in the Ruler, and a clutching anxiety of scores of millions who demanded and awaited orders.

Since then there has been no lack of orders. Although the Dictatorship is veiled by constitutional forms, it is none the less effective. Great things have been done, and greater attempted. To compare Roosevelt's effort with that of Hitler is to insult not Roosevelt but civilisation. The petty persecutions and old-world assertions of brutality in which the German idol has indulged only show their smallness and squalor compared to the **renaissance** of creative effort with which the name of Roosevelt will always be associated.

Winston Churchill, *Great Contemporaries*, 1937, Fontana ed., 1959.

(ii) An American historian suggests that the New Deal brought about revolutionary changes.

A revolution was started by the New Deal – not a revolution in the violent, turbulent sense, but a revolution nevertheless. The whole concept of the state, or national government, underwent a **metamorphosis**. . . . Now it became the **interventionist state**. It imposed on the free business enterpriser all sorts of controls and regulations; it entered openly into business itself, often as competitor with private corporations; it used its great fiscal and financial powers to redistribute wealth and to create income; it committed itself to an elaborate program of social security that offered protection, in time, to the whole population against the mischances of unemployment, invalidity, and sudden death, and from the cradle to the grave. . . .

And political power, too, had shifted. Previously political power had been in the hands of the middle class – the industrialists, the bankers, the larger farmers. Now political power was concentrating more and more in the hands of the workers.

Louis Hacker, *The Shaping of the American Tradition*, Columbia University Press, 1947.

(iii) A British historian throws doubt on the success of the New Deal.

The shortcomings of the New Deal are very evident to historians today. Unemployment remained obstinately high. It fell from some 15 million in 1933 to under 8 million in 1937 but it rose again to 9½ million in 1939. In fact Roosevelt's administrations failed to 'cure' the blight and waste of human resources until the United States geared industry to war. But the attitude of the President and administration, brilliantly publicized, gave renewed hope to the nation and provided leadership without the destruction of democracy. There is thus a stark contrast between the general psychological impact of the New Deal, and the real success of the many different laws, special agencies and programmes which constituted it.

J. A. S. Grenville, *A World History of the Twentieth Century*, Vol. 1: *Western Dominance, 1900–45*, Fontana, 1980.

Glossary

curtailment reduction
emblazoned clearly marked
interventionist state a state where the government influences the economy; for example, investing money in

projects to create employment
jurisdiction legal authority
metamorphosis complete change
peroration end of a speech
renaissance revival

Questions

1 Read Source A and explain in your own words the meaning of the term 'New Deal'. How important do you think such slogans are?
2 Read Sources B and C and decide with which of the following statements you can agree. Give reasons for your decision.
 (i) Roosevelt believed that government had a responsibility to reduce the level of unemployment.
 (ii) Roosevelt believed that poverty in the USA was more the result of the nervousness than the incompetence of American businessmen.
 (iii) The problems facing Roosevelt were serious and urgent.
3 Do you think the special occasion is reflected in the content of the President's speech in Source B? Give reasons for your answer.
4 Study Source D and, also using your own knowledge, explain: (a) who are represented by the man leading the procession, the donkey, the man in the top hat, the elephants; (b) what message do you think that the cartoonist is conveying?
5 Read Source E and make a list of all the improvements mentioned in it.
 (a) Explain how each of these improvements depended upon the others for their effectiveness (for example, how the building of dams related to the supply of electricity).
 (b) Explain how these connected improvements were achieved.
 (c) How reliable do you think the information in this extract is?
6 How do Sources E and F help us to understand the TVA project?
7 Read Source G. Do you think that this is propaganda for or against Roosevelt? Give your reasons.
8 Study Source H. What evidence is there that the New Deal had only a temporary effect in improving the level of unemployment?
9 Compare Sources I(i), (ii) and (iii).
 (a) Explain how the writers differ from each other in judging: (i) the effects of the New Deal; (ii) the personal importance of Roosevelt.
 (b) What do you think the reasons are for these differences?

Chapter 15 Great Britain: the Welfare State

How far should government use taxes to help the poor and needy? There is much disagreement about this today: some people think that the government does too much; and others think that not enough is done to help the poor, the sick, the disabled, and old and the unemployed. Which side is right?

Introduction

It is important to understand the origins of our present Welfare State. During the 1930s many people in Britain were poor, unemployed or both. The poor received little help from the government in the form, for example, of unemployment benefit (the 'dole'). Furthermore, in order to obtain the dole people were often investigated to find out if they really needed help. This investigation was called 'the means test' and was deeply resented.

During the Second World War many people, including politicians, members of the armed services and the general public, began to believe that conditions should be improved after the war – that the people who had suffered and sacrificed so much should be treated rather better by the government. As a basis for post-war planning, William Beveridge produced a report in 1942, called *Social Insurance and Allied Services* and usually known as the Beveridge Report. It proposed a complete system of social insurance to protect people against the effects of poverty 'from the cradle to the grave'.

The proposals were eagerly discussed. Some people supported them wholeheartedly, believing that money should be found for a health service, better education, better unemployment benefits and old age pensions, for example. On the other hand, some people doubted whether the large sums of money required could be found. The doubters also believed that too much government help could destroy the idea that people should do as much as possible to help themselves. The Labour Government of 1945–50 put most of Beveridge's schemes into operation. But the debate about the Welfare State continues.

A The Beveridge Report

An extract from the Report. Sir William (later Lord) Beveridge was a senior civil servant who had helped to plan the early welfare schemes before the First World War.

The aim of the Plan for Social Security is to abolish want by ensuring that every citizen willing to serve according to his powers has at all times an income sufficient to meet his responsibilities . . . want was a needless scandal due to not taking the trouble to prevent it. . . .

The first principle is that any proposals for the future should not be restricted by **consideration of sectional interests**. . . .

Social insurance fully developed may provide income security; it is an attack on Want. But Want is only one of the five giants on the road of reconstruction and in some ways the easiest to attack. The others are Disease, Ignorance, Squalor and Idleness. . . .

Social Security must be achieved by co-operation between the State and the individual. . . . The State in organising security should not stifle incentive, opportunity, responsibility; in establishing a national minimum, it should leave room and encouragement for voluntary action by each individual to provide more than that minimum for himself and his family.

Social Insurance and Allied Services, HMSO, 1942.

B An assessment of reaction to the Beveridge Report

The Ministry of Information produced this assessment in March 1943, after the Report had become a 'best seller'.

Interest in the Beveridge Plan on its publication was really tremendous. For a week or two the war news tended to take a back seat and one report says: 'There has been possibly more widespread discussion on this than on any single event since the outbreak of the war.' The publicity given to the scheme by the radio and Press together with the explanatory pamphlets on the subject, which appeared almost overnight, aroused a quite remarkable enthusiasm.

Practically everyone approved of the underlying principles, and hopes ran high that the Plan would be put into operation as soon as possible. . . .

Soldiers writing home spoke of their pleasure at the Scheme, saying, 'This gives us some heart to fight. We know that if something happens to us our wives and children will never want.'

To the critics who inquired 'Can we pay for it?' the impatient reply was given, 'We can always pay for wars, this one costs £15 million a day. We will just *have* to afford the Beveridge Plan.'

Quoted in J. Beveridge, *Beveridge and his Plan*, Hodder & Stoughton, 1954.

C The government view in 1943

Sir John Anderson, a Conservative member of Churchill's War Cabinet and soon to be Chancellor of the Exchequer, is being reported by a Radical-Liberal MP, T. L. Horabin.

The only test of [the Government's] **integrity** . . . is whether they are prepared or not to give the unemployed pay at **subsistence level** the whole time they are unemployed. They are not. Speaking in the Beveridge debate on the 16th February, 1943, Sir John Anderson said:

Sir William Beveridge proposes that after a period of unconditional unemployment benefit, which he has fixed, subject to certain adjustments, at six months, an unemployed person should be able to continue to draw unemployment benefit, subject to attendance at a work or training centre. . . . The training schemes would not, however, in the view of the Government, constitute an effective safeguard against the abuse of unemployment benefit, and the Government consider that it would be vitally necessary to introduce some system which would provide a strong check against such abuse. A similar problem arises in respect of disability benefit, and here, too, some means will have to be found to check the abuses inseparable from any system of benefit of fixed amount and unlimited duration. It is the Government's considered opinion that both unemployment and disability benefit will have to be made of limited duration, although the period need not necessarily be the same in every case. . . .

The other **fundamental principle** laid down by Sir William Beveridge, without the adoption of which want could not be abolished, was that all allowances should rise or fall with the cost of living. If allowances are fixed and the cost of living goes up, they at once become inadequate and hardship results, as old age pensioners know to their cost.

This principle also the Government rejected out of hand.

T. L. Horabin, *Politics Made Plain: What the Next General Election will Really be About*, Penguin, 1944.

D The Education Act, 1944

Lord Butler remembers how, as President of the Board of Education (later to become the Ministry of Education), he was responsible for introducing the Act.

All the basic educational reforms, such as raising the leaving age, abolishing fees in the maintained secondary schools and so on, had already been agreed by all parties concerned, especially the National Union of Teachers and the Trades Union Congress. . . . Most of my time had been spent negotiating a diplomatic solution to the problem of the relationship of state and church schools. The object of the Bill was completely to reorganise education into primary and secondary schooling, which would be free for all parents except for those who wished to pay for their children to attend the independent (public) schools. Within this framework it was proposed that **denominational schools** should choose between being 'aided' or 'controlled'. The government grant for 'aided' schools was to be fifty per cent towards alterations to bring the premises up to the prescribed standards and on repairs to the interior.

In addition to the practical establishment of schools, the Act contained some religious points for the first time in history. The school day was to begin with an act of worship and there was to be universal religious instruction in all schools on the basis of an agreed syllabus. . . .

R. A. Butler, *The Art of Memory: Friends in Perspective*, Hodder & Stoughton, 1982.

E 'Let Us Face the Future'

Part of the Labour Party Manifesto for the 1945 General Election, which it won by a large majority.

The Labour Party has played a leading part in the long campaign for proper social security for all – social provision against rainy days to a minimum. Labour led the fight against the mean and shabby treatment which was the lot of millions while Conservative Governments were in power over long years. A Labour Government will press on rapidly with **legislation** extending social insurance over the necessary wide field to all.

But the great national programmes of education, health and social services are costly things. Only an efficient and prosperous nation can afford them in full measure. If, unhappily, bad times were to come, and our opponents were in power, then, running true to form, they would be likely to cut these social provisions on the plea that the nation could not meet the cost. That was the line they adopted on at least three occasions between the wars.

There is no good reason why Britain should not afford such programmes, but she will need full employment and the highest possible industrial efficiency in order to do so.

Quoted in F. Bealey, *The Social and Political Thought of the British Labour Party*, Weidenfeld & Nicolson, 1970.

F The National Insurance Bill, February 1946

Prime Minister Clement Attlee speaking in the House of Commons on the Bill which was one of the first reforms in the Labour Party's Welfare State Programme.

The question is asked – Can we afford it [the National Insurance Bill]? Supposing the answer is 'No'? What does that mean? It really means that the sum total of goods produced and the services rendered by the people of this country is not sufficient to provide for all our people at all times, in sickness, in health, in youth, and in age, the very modest standard of life that is represented by the sums of money set out in the Second Schedule to this Bill. I cannot believe that our national productivity is so slow, that our willingness to work is so feeble or that we can submit to the world that the masses of our people must be condemned to **penury**. . . . the only validity for the claim that we cannot afford it must rest either on there not being enough in the **pool,** or on the claim that some sections of society have a priority to take out so much that the others must suffer want.

I am not prepared to admit either of these propositions.

Hansard, fifth series, vol. 418, HMSO, 1946.

G A cartoon from the magazine *Punch*, 1949

H The controversy over the National Health Service

Aneurin Bevan, Minister of Health, 1945–51 and a firm believer in the National Health Service, remembers the controversy.

When the Service started and the demands for spectacles, dental attention and drugs rocketed upwards the pessimists said: 'We told you so. The people cannot be trusted to use the Service prudently or intelligently. It is bad now but there is worse to come. Abuse will crowd on abuse until the whole scheme collapses.' . . .

The first few estimates for the Health Service seemed to justify the critics. Expenditure exceeded the estimates by huge amounts, and Mr Churchill with his usual lack of restraint plunged into the attack. In this he showed less insight than his colleagues, who watched his antics with increasing alarm. They knew the Service was already popular with the people. If the Service could be killed they would not mind, but they would wish it done more stealthily and in such a fashion that they would not appear to have the responsibility.

Ordinary men and women were aware of what was happening. They knew from their own experience that a considerable proportion of the initial expenditure, especially on dentistry and spectacles, was the result of past neglect. When the first rush was over the demand would even out. And so it proved. Indeed, it was proved even beyond the expectations of those of us who had most faith in the Service.

Aneurin Bevan, *In Place of Fear*, Macgibbon & Kee, 1952, Quartet Books ed., 1978.

I(i) The Conservative Party and the National Health Service Bill

An amendment proposed by the Conservatives on the second reading of the Bill, 30 April 1946.

This House, while wishing to establish a comprehensive health service, declines to give a Second Reading to a Bill which **prejudices** the patient's right to an independent family doctor; which retards the development of the hospital services by destroying local ownership, and gravely menaces all charitable foundations by diverting to purposes other than those intended by the donors the trust funds of the voluntary hospitals; and which weakens the responsibility of local authorities without planning the health services as a whole.

Hansard, fifth series, vol. 422, HMSO, 1946.

I(ii) The British Medical Association (BMA) and the National Health Service

The author of this extract has referred to various issues of the *British Medical Journal* to assess the reaction of the BMA (the professional organisation of doctors) to the National Health Service.

On January 8, 1948, six months before the Service was due to go into operation, a special representative meeting of the BMA **unanimously** passed a resolution in which they solemnly declared that 'in their considered opinion the National Health Service Act, 1946, in its present form is so grossly at variance with the essential principles of our profession that it should be rejected absolutely by all practitioners'. A month later a **plebi-scite** of the profession asked the question, 'Do you approve or disapprove, of the National Health Service Act, 1946, in its present form?' In an 84 per cent poll a nine-to-one majority voted disapproval. A month after this a representative meeting of the BMA decided unanimously not to enter the new Service on July 5 unless substantial changes were made in the Act. 'Now, BMA, stand firm!' exhorted a correspondent in the Journal of the BMA after this vote. 'The profession has spoken in no uncertain voice. . . . We are all behind you and expect a lead. Don't give way or compromise – it is too dangerous. . . . Our patients look to us to refuse service under the Act as it stands and to maintain our professional freedom. Think of what public apathy cost Germany in the '30s. We must cling to our liberty.'

Pauline Gregg, *The Welfare State*, Harrap, 1967.

J Looking back

This extract is oral evidence from Dr John Wigg speaking in the 1960s. He is looking back to the time of the introduction of the Health Service.

One of the things which made me wholeheartedly in favour of the Health Service was that I knew that unless a service which did not depend upon money passing at the time of the consultation was established, it was impossible to have a fully comprehensive service. I think the benefits to the doctor have not been sufficiently appreciated. I'm quite sure that the medical profession has never really been wholeheartedly in favour of the Health Service ever since it started. I remember one case, . . . er, how my treatment was terribly interrupted. I had been looking after a child with pneumonia and I saw it about two or three times at the beginning of the week and I hoped it might be better on the Thursday – of course you always had to hope then, because there weren't any antibiotics – and I went up to see it, and, . . . er, the child was gone! The only person left was an elder sister of the child, so I said, 'where is the child and where is your mother', and she said, 'well, doctor, she took it off to the hospital, you see, really we hadn't any more money and we didn't know quite what to do.'

The Making of the Welfare State (from a recording), Longman, 1966.

K(i) The number of people receiving pensions and benefits, 1950–69

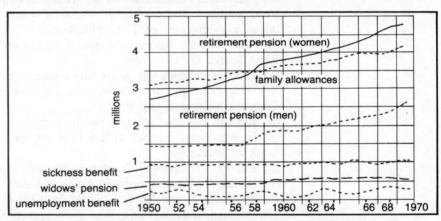

Central Statistical Office, in A. F. Sillitoe, *Britain in Figures: A Handbook of Social Statistics*, Penguin, 1971.

K(ii) The percentage of the country's wealth (Gross National Product) spent on various items of expenditure 1952–69

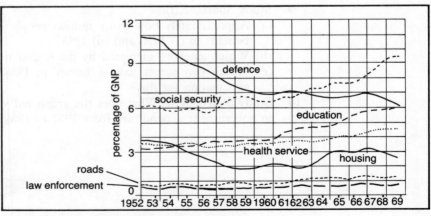

Central Statistical Office, in Sillitoe, *Britain in Figures*.

Glossary

consideration of sectional interests favouring some groups or classes in society over others
denominational schools schools run by the churches
fundamental principle most important guiding rule
integrity honesty
legislation making laws

penury poverty
plebiscite vote by all members
pool here, money from taxes and the proposed national insurance contributions
prejudices has a bad effect upon
subsistence level just enough to live
unanimously with everyone agreeing

Questions

1 Read Source A. Decide which of the following statements you can agree with. Explain the reasons for your decisions.
   (i) Beveridge believed that people had been poor because Britain had insufficient wealth to prevent poverty.
   (ii) Beveridge believed that his suggested reforms were more likely to be adopted because of the Second World War.
   (iii) Beveridge foresaw the problem of lazy people 'spongeing' on the Welfare State.

2 Imagine that you are a soldier or a member of the ATS (a woman soldier). Using Sources A and B and your own knowledge, write a letter to the MP for your home constituency to persuade him to support the Beveridge Plan.

3 Read Source C and explain in your own words:
   (a) what is the view of T. L. Horabin;
   (b) how Sir John Anderson's view disagrees with Horabin's.

4 Read Source D.
   (a) List the changes which are mentioned in the extract.
   (b) Which one do you consider most important? Give your reasons.

5 Compare Sources E and F.
   (a) Explain the connection between them.
   (b) In what ways do they differ? How do you explain the differences?

6 Look at Source G.
   (a) Explain the cartoonist's attitude towards the Welfare State.
   (b) Explain briefly the opposite point of view.

7 Read Sources H and I(i) and (ii). Make a list of all the arguments in these extracts against various aspects of the proposed National Health Service and explain which argument or arguments you think were most justified.

8 Read Source J. Why was this doctor in favour of the NHS?

9 Study Source K(i).
   (a) Approximately how many million people were receiving pensions and benefits in (i) 1950 and (ii) 1968?
   (b) Which category increased by the largest number from 1950 to 1968?
   (c) Which two curves have a 'bump' in 1958? What do you think is the explanation for this?

10 Study Source K(ii). What does the graph tell you about changing priorities in government expenditure from 1952 to 1969?

Part 4   Nationalism

Chapter 16 India: independence and partition

When India became independent in 1947 the country was partitioned to create the state of Pakistan and very many people were killed in communal riots and clashes. Was Britain therefore right to agree to partition?

Introduction

During the period between about 1880 and 1960 the empires of the European countries were larger than ever before and the British Empire was the biggest of them all. The most impressive part of that empire was India, often referred to as 'the jewel in the crown'. From 1877 to 1947 the monarch of England was also Empress/Emperor of India.

However, many Indians wanted to govern themselves. These nationalists formed the Indian National Congress to work for Indian independence. A number of them were lawyers, educated and trained in Britain. But they gradually realised that they must emphasise Indian culture in their campaign if India was to be truly free of British control. The most famous of these nationalist leaders was Mahatma Gandhi. The demonstrations which he organised were so successful that by about 1930 the British Government had to consider seriously India's demand for independence.

There were, however, reasons why the British delayed responding to these demands. The approaching war meant that it was important for Britain to keep India as part of her empire. There was also the problem of religion. The majority of Indians were Hindus, though a large minority

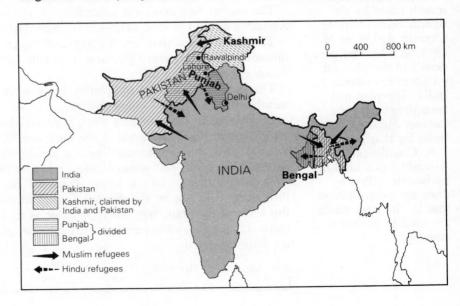

India
Pakistan
Kashmir, claimed by India and Pakistan
Punjab ⎱ divided
Bengal ⎰
→ Muslim refugees
←--- Hindu refugees

were Muslims. As the prospect of independence came closer, the Muslims feared that they would be discriminated against by the Hindus. The Muslim League therefore came to demand the partition of India and the creation of a separate Muslim state of Pakistan.

The intense desire to be rid of British rule and the mounting hatred and fear between Hindus and Muslims led to the outbreak of widespread violence by 1947.

A   A speech by the President of the Muslim League

Mohamed Ali Jinnah speaking at Lahore in what was then northern India, 22 March 1940.

'Musalmans' is another word for Muslims.

. . . it is a dream that the Hindus and Muslims can ever evolve a common nationality, and this **misconception** of one Indian nation has gone far beyond the limits and is the cause of most of your troubles and will lead India to destruction if we fail to revise our notions in time. The Hindus and Muslims belong to two different religions, philosophies, social customs, literatures. They neither intermarry nor **interdine** together and, indeed, they belong to two different civilizations which are based mainly on conflicting ideas and conceptions. Their aspects on life and of life are different. It is quite clear that Hindus and Musalmans derive their inspiration from different sources of history. . . . To yoke together two such nations under a single State, one as a numerical minority and the other as a majority, must lead to growing discontent and final destruction of any fabric that may be so built up for the government of such a nation. . . . Musalmans are a nation according to any definition of a nation, and they must have their homelands, their territory and their State.

Quoted in J. Ahmad, *Some Recent Speeches and Writings of Mr Jinnah*, vol. 1, Lahore, 1952.

B   The plan for giving independence to India

This is a report of a speech made by the British Prime Minister, Clement Attlee, in May 1946, in which he gave details of the plan for giving independence to India. The plan had been drawn up by a Cabinet Mission sent to India for that purpose.

A 'Constituent Assembly' is a kind of parliament called to draw up a constitution, that is, the laws which are used to govern a country.

The new plan for India consists of three parts. One lays down the broad lines on which a future constitution should be based.

The second lays down the procedure for electing an Indian Constituent Assembly to meet as soon as possible in New Delhi and draft a constitution.

The third states that the Viceroy will proceed immediately with the formation of an **interim** Government to rule India while the new constitution is being drawn up.

The new India can be completely independent or can choose to be a member of the British Commonwealth. . . .

Pakistan is, in the Mission's view, impracticable. Such a Pakistan would comprise two main areas, one in the north-west and one in the north-east. Yet the north-west areas would have a non-Moslem minority of 37.93 per cent and the north-east a non-Moslem minority of 48.31 per cent.

New minority problems would therefore be created. The individual Provinces could not be sub-divided to cut out these inner minorities. . . . But short of Pakistan, very full recognition is made of Moslem claims. The cultural, religious, economic and other interests of non-Hindu communities are fully protected.

News Chronicle, 17 May 1946.

C The British Prime Minister speaks again about independence for India

Clement Attlee made this statement on 3 June 1947.

When he speaks of 'one or two successor authorities' at the end of the statement he is referring to the new governments which will take over from the British.

On 20 February 1947, His Majesty's Government announced their intention of transferring power in British India to Indian hands by June 1948. His Majesty's Government had hoped that it would be possible for the major parties to co-operate in the working-out of the Cabinet Mission Plan of 16 May 1946, and evolve for India a constitution acceptable to all concerned. This hope has not been fulfilled. . . .

. . . the Muslim League Party . . . has decided not to participate in the Constituent Assembly.

It has always been the desire of His Majesty's Government that power should be transferred in accordance with the wishes of the Indian people themselves. This task would have been greatly **facilitated** if there had been agreement among the Indian political parties. In the absence of such agreement, the task of devising a method by which the wishes of the Indian people can be ascertained has **devolved upon** His Majesty's Government. . . .

The major political parties have repeatedly emphasized their desire that there should be the earliest possible transfer of power in India. With this desire His Majesty's Government are in full sympathy, and they are willing to anticipate the date of June 1948, for the handing over of power by the setting up of an independent Indian Government or Governments at an even earlier date. Accordingly, as the most **expeditious**, and indeed the only practicable way of meeting this desire, His Majesty's Government propose to introduce legislation during the current session for the transfer of power this year on a **Dominion** Status basis to one or two successor authorities according to the decisions taken as a result of this announcement.

Quoted in V. P. Menon, *Transfer of Power in India*, Orient Longman, 1957.

D Massacres

(i) The massacres in Bihar in north-eastern India, November 1946, described by General Sir Francis Tuker, a British officer serving in India.

Of all the terrible doings of 1946, this was the most shocking. Great mobs of Hindus turned suddenly, but with every preparation for the deed, upon the few Muslims who had lived, and whose forefathers had lived, in **amity** and trust, all their lives, among these very Hindu neighbours. It has never been ascertained who was the organizing brain of this well-laid, widely-planned plot of **extirpation**. All that we do know is that it went to a fixed plan and schedule. Had it not been so, such large mobs, fully armed with prepared weapons, would never have collected in the time and moved with such obvious, **fiendish** intent from victim to victim. The number of Muslim dead, men, women, and children, in this short, savage killing was about 7,000 to 8,000. Women and their babies were cut up, butchered, with an obscene devilry.

General Sir Francis Tuker, *While Memory Serves*, Cassell, 1950.

(ii) The massacre of Sikhs by Muslims in the Rawalpindi area (soon to be part of Pakistan), described by General Sir Frank Messervy, a British officer serving in India.

'Memsahib' is a courteous title given to a European married lady.

... I remember an officer's wife arriving by train. The train had been stopped outside Chaklala and she heard shrieks and groans (the time was just about dawn). She lowered a shutter, and looked out, to find Sikhs being dragged out of the carriages and hacked to pieces by the side of the line. She was horrified and screamed, whereupon one of the band came up to her carriage and said 'Don't be frightened, Memsahib, nobody will harm you. We've just got this job to do, and then the train will go on.'

Quoted in I. Stephens, *Pakistan: Old Country, New Nation*, Ernest Benn, 1963, Penguin ed., 1964.

E The problems facing Lord Mountbatten as Viceroy

Lord Mountbatten was the last Viceroy of India and was given the task of ensuring that the transition to self-government went smoothly. Here an historian describes his address to the Royal Empire Society in London on 6 October 1948 after he had returned from India.

Mountbatten's assignment was to take Britain out of India by June, 1948. In order to give the British Parliament time to debate and pass the legislation necessary for this reduction of the Empire, the solution had to be ready by the end of 1947. But on the spot, he and his advisers agreed that this timetable would be too slow; things were happening too quickly. . . . 'I arrived out there,' Mountbatten told his audience, 'to find this terrible pendulum of massacres swinging wider and wider.

'Personally, I was convinced that the right solution for then and still would have been to keep a United India,' under the plan of May 16, 1946, Mountbatten revealed. But this presupposed co-operation between the two parties. 'Mr. Jinnah,' however, Mountbatten stated, 'made it abundantly clear from the first moment that so long as he lived he would never accept a United India. He demanded partition, he insisted on Pakistan. Congress, on the other hand, favored an undivided country, but the Congress leaders agreed that they would accept partition to avoid civil war. Mountbatten 'was convinced that the Moslem League would have fought.'

But Congress, said Mountbatten, refused to let large non-Moslem areas go to Pakistan. 'That automatically meant a partition of the great provinces of the Punjab and Bengal,' so that their non-Moslem areas would not be incorporated into Moslem Pakistan. 'When I told Mr. Jinnah,' Mountbatten confided to the Royal Empire Society, 'that I had their [Congress's] provisional agreement to partition he was overjoyed. When I said it logically followed that this would involve partition of the Punjab and Bengal he was horrified. He produced the strongest arguments why these provinces should not be partitioned. He said they had national characteristics and that partition would be disastrous. I agreed, but said how much more must I now feel that the same considerations applied to the partitioning of the whole of India. He did not like that, and started explaining why India had to be partitioned, and so we went round and round the mulberry bush until finally he realized that either he could have a United India with an unpartitioned Punjab and Bengal or a divided India with a partitioned Punjab and Bengal, and he finally accepted the latter solution.'

Louis Fischer, *Gandhi: His Life and Message for the World*, Mentor Books, 1954.

F Jawaharlal Nehru, first Prime Minister of India, welcomes independence

Nehru is speaking to the Constituent Assembly, 14 August 1947.

At the stroke of the midnight hour, when the world sleeps, India will awake to life and freedom. A moment comes, which comes but rarely in history, when we step out from the old to the new, when an age ends, and when the soul of a nation, long suppressed, finds utterance. It is fitting that at this solemn moment we take the pledge of dedication to the service of India and her people and to the still larger cause of humanity. . . .

Freedom and power bring responsibility. The responsibility rests upon this assembly, a sovereign body representing the sovereign people of India. Before the birth of freedom we have endured all the pains of labour and our hearts are heavy with the memory of this sorrow. Some of those pains continue even now. Nevertheless, the past is over and it is the future that beckons to us now.

Quoted in S. Gopal (ed.), *Jawaharlal Nehru: An Anthology*, OUP, 1980.

G Independence Day

A British newspaper comments on the event.

SALUTE
Today marks an event which future generations will unquestionably regard as one of the most significant in modern history – the formal transfer of power, by a smooth, free and voluntary process, from Britain to the two new Dominions of India and Pakistan.

This change has been achieved with far less bloodshed and strife than had been feared. As a result, the good name of Britain stands higher today in India and the Far East than for many generations past.

Such a voluntary transfer, in the words of Mr. Jinnah, the new Governor-General of Pakistan, is 'unknown in the world's history.' 'We mark our deep appreciation,' he says, 'of Mr. Attlee, His Majesty's Government and Parliament, and the British nation.'

This is indeed an almost miraculously happy conclusion to the story of Anglo-Indian relations. Let us therefore salute today the two new Dominions, and wish all future success and prosperity to the Indian peoples, in growing friendship with Britain. And let us congratulate all those, the Prime Minister and Lord Mountbatten especially, who have thus achieved a feat of practical statesmanship unique in modern times.

Daily Herald, 15 August 1947.

H The assassination of Mahatma Gandhi

Prime Minister Jawaharlal Nehru announces the news on All India Radio, 30 January 1948.

Friends and comrades, the light has gone out of our lives and there is darkness everywhere and I do not quite know what to tell you and how to say it. Our beloved leader, Bapu as we called him, the Father of the Nation is no more. Perhaps I am wrong to say that. Nevertheless, we will not see him again as we have seen him for these many years. We will not run to him for advice and seek **solace** from him and that is a terrible blow not to me only but to millions and millions in this country. And it is a little difficult to soften the blow by any advice that I or anyone else can give you. . . .

A mad man has put an end to his life, for I can only call him mad who did it, and yet there has been enough of poison spread in this country during the past years and months and this poison has had an effect on people's minds. We must face this poison. We must root out this poison and we must face all the perils that **encompass** us and face them not madly or badly but rather in the way that our beloved leader taught us to face them. The first thing to remember now is that no one of us dare misbehave because we are angry. We have to behave like strong determined people, determined to face all the perils that surround us, determined to carry out the **mandate** that our great teacher, and our great leader, has given us, and remembering always if, as I really believe, his spirit looks upon us and sees us nothing would displease him so much as to see that we have indulged in unseemly behaviour or in violence.

Quoted in S. L. Poplai (ed.), *India, 1947–1950*, OUP.

Glossary

amity friendship
devolved upon fallen to
Dominion self-governing member of the British Commonwealth
encompass surround
expeditious fast
extirpation extermination
facilitated made easier

fiendish cruel, evil
foe enemy
interdine eat in each other's company
interim temporary
mandate command
misconception misunderstanding
solace comfort

Questions

1 Read Sources A and B. Explain in what ways and why the attitudes of Jinnah and Attlee were different.

2 From the evidence in Source B and from your own knowledge explain in your own words: (a) the meaning of the word 'Viceroy' and who the Viceroy was at the time; (b) why a Constituent Assembly was necessary.

3 Compare Sources B and C. In what ways had the British Government shifted its ground on the granting of independence between May 1946 and June 1947?

4 Does the evidence in Sources D(i), D(ii) and E justify the British Government's change of plans as described in Source C? Give the reasons for your answer.

5 Look at Source F. What does it tell us about Nehru's feelings about (a) the colonial period; (b) independence and the future?

6 Did the readers of the *Daily Herald* (Source G) obtain a completely accurate picture of Indian independence? Explain the reasons for your answer.

7 Read Source H. What does this tell you about (a) the importance of Gandhi and (b) the problem of violence at the time? What other evidence is there in this chapter about these two matters?

8 Using information from all the sources say why you think the British Government agreed to the creation of the separate state of Pakistan. Do you consider that its decision was justified?

Chapter 17 Hungary: the uprising of 1956

In 1956 the Hungarian people rose up in revolt against their Soviet-controlled government and a new independent government was set up. But Soviet tanks returned to crush the uprising. Had the USSR any right to do this?

Introduction

During the late 1940s Communist parties, with the support of the Soviet Union, took control of most of the countries of eastern Europe. In fact, the USSR came to have such an influence in these states that in the west they were called Soviet 'satellites' – it was as if they were controlled by the USSR as the movement of the moon is controlled by the earth. Moreover, the men who became the leaders of the east European governments were supporters of Stalin, the Soviet dictator, and they set about establishing strong control over their states as Stalin had in the USSR. For example, they set up powerful secret police organisations, imprisoned their opponents and insisted on loyalty to Moscow. This Soviet domination was deeply resented by many people in the east European states and there was a great deal of discontent and unrest. Then in 1953 Stalin died and Khrushchev, the new Soviet leader, wanted more liberal policies.

In Hungary the Stalinist party leader was Matyas Rakosi (pronounced rah-koshee). He built up a strong police, the AVO (the initials stand for 'State Security Department'), who imprisoned opponents of the government and were deeply hated by many Hungarians. But in February 1956 the Soviet leader, Khrushchev, made a speech in which he bitterly criticised Stalin. Many people in eastern Europe, including Hungary, took this as a sign that they could have freer governments. In July the hated Rakosi was forced to resign. By October, in an increasingly tense atmosphere, students started to agitate for the appointment of Imre Nagy (pronounced nodge) as leader of the government. He had been an opponent of Rakosi. On 23 October in the capital, Budapest, an angry crowd destroyed the statue of Stalin; and the government called in Soviet tanks to restore order. The next day, 24 October, Nagy was appointed prime minister. For the next month bitter fighting took place. The Hungarians were desperate to keep their new independence; the Soviets were determined to crush the government of Nagy, who threatened to remove Hungary from the Warsaw Pact – the Soviet military alliance. But the ill-armed Hungarian people were no match for tanks. The uprising was crushed and Nagy taken away and executed.

A   The destruction of Stalin's statue in Budapest, 23 October 1956

B   The views of Hungarians

(i) A Budapest student.

The peasants' and workers' sons were the most outspoken. They were more insolent than those of middle-class origin. They could ask questions like, 'Isn't the delivery quota too high?'. . . It was perhaps the peasant kids, who went home regularly and saw the misery in the village, who were most outspoken in their criticism.

(ii) A middle-aged worker in a Budapest shoe factory.

There was a general discontent among the workers and it came out whenever two people began to talk. The workers did not believe in anything the communists promised them, because the communists had cheated on their promises so often.

(iii) A factory worker from Csepel, a steel-making town near Budapest.

The communists nationalised all the factories and similar enterprises, proclaiming the slogan, 'The factory is yours – you work for yourself'. Exactly the opposite of this was true. They promised us everything, at the same time **subjugating** us and pulling us down to the greatest misery conceivable.

(iv) A communist sympathiser recalling his experiences in 1952–53.

Then I went to Csepel and built socialism there too, as an iron worker in the Matyas Rakosi works. It was there that I realised how much the workers hated the régime. . . . The workers hated the régime to such an extent that by 1953 they were ready to destroy it and everything that went with it.

Quoted in B. Lomax, *Hungary 1956*, Allison & Busby, 1976.

C Broadcasts from Budapest radio, 25 October

A British journalist reports on the news bulletins.
'G.M.T.' is Greenwich Mean Time, that is, London time. Hungarian time is one hour later.

Budapest radio yesterday broadcast the following:-

07.40 (G.M.T.). – Announcement by the Defence Minister appealing to all members of the Army who for any reason had been cut off from their units to report back immediately.

Announcements were then made at regular intervals, stating that the Budapest **curfew** remained in force between 18.00 and 06.00 hours and ordering all citizens to keep their front doors locked. There were apologies for long queues and difficulty in making telephone calls. The Government was doing its best to maintain bread supplies, but the sale of spirits was forbidden. More trams and buses were said to be on the streets.

08.15. – Order of the day by the Defence Minister announcing that in the great battles that had taken place heavy losses had been inflicted on the counter-revolutionary gangs, that many prisoners had been taken, and that protection had been heroically given to the citizens of Budapest against destruction and looting. With the aid of units of the **fraternal** Soviet Army they had, by their self-sacrificing fighting, secured the defence of the achievements of the 'people's democracy' and the people's power. The Minister ordered the troops of the 'people's army' finally to **liquidate** by midday the **insurrectionary** forces still in Budapest.

SHOOTING CONTINUES

09.47. – Announcement that, though the restoration of order was making good progress, certain irresponsible elements or small groups were still trying to create disturbances and, what was more, were firing shots. The Government was making a firm stand against such happenings.

The Times, 26 October 1956.

D Prime Minister Imre Nagy asks for help

The Prime Minister of Hungary sent this telegram to the Secretary-General of the United Nations, 1 November 1956.
The 'Warsaw Treaty' is a military pact uniting the forces of the USSR and its east European allies.
The 'four great powers' were the USA, the UK, France and (non-communist) China – the permanent members (with the USSR) of the UN Security Council.

Reliable reports have reached the government of the Hungarian People's Republic that further Soviet units are entering Hungary. The President of the Council of Ministers in his capacity of Minister of Foreign Affairs summoned M. Andropov, Ambassador Extraordinary and **Plenipotentiary** of the Soviet Union to Hungary, and expressed his strongest protest against the entry of further Soviet troops into Hungary. He demanded the instant and immediate withdrawal of these Soviet forces. He informed the Soviet Ambassador that the Hungarian government immediately repudiates the Warsaw Treaty and at the same time declares Hungary's neutrality, turns to the United Nations, and requests the help of the four great powers in defending the country's neutrality. The Government of the Hungarian People's Republic made the Declaration of Neutrality on 1 November 1956; therefore I request your Excellency to put on the agenda of the forthcoming General Assembly of the United Nations the question of Hungary's neutrality and the defence of this neutrality by the four great powers.

Quoted in H. Hanak, *Soviet Foreign Policy Since the Death of Stalin*, Routledge & Kegan Paul, 1972.

E   Paul Ignotus comments on the manhunts for 'Ávós' men

He was a Hungarian writer who was imprisoned by AVO (political police) 1949–56. He was released during the uprising and later escaped to Britain.

'Ávós' were members of the AVO. 'Péter' was the general in charge of the AVO.

Uglier even than these [scenes of violent demonstration] were the manhunts and the lynchings. 'Ávós, ávós! – *Ávó*-man! – the howl went up, and the unfortunate victim of mob hatred was shot or beaten to death on the spot, and sometimes hanged upside down, with one or two hysterical women spitting at the corpse. Once lynch law takes over, innocents are bound to suffer: who in that turmoil could ascertain whether the man singled out for vengeance was really an 'ávós'? Even if found in the hated, blue-lapelled uniform, he might have been innocent; quite a number of poor lads had been recruited willy-nilly for the force. Moreover, the most notorious thugs of the Stalinist years had, by the outbreak of the revolt, already been imprisoned (Péter, etc.), or at any rate moved into less conspicuous positions. As is always the case: the innocent or the little crook caught on the spot was made to pay for the absent master scoundrels.

Paul Ignotus, *Hungary*, Ernest Benn, 1972.

F   'The Murder of Hungary'

This article describing the situation in Hungary appeared in a British newspaper.

BUDAPEST CRUSHED – Red troops storm into Parliament
THE MURDER OF HUNGARY
Nagy marched out at gunpoint.
From JEFFREY BLYTH: On the Austro-Hungarian Frontier, Sunday Night

HUNGARY, the little country that dared to defy Russia, was murdered today. Russian troops struck at the freedom fighters all over the country. More than 1,000 tanks surrounded Budapest. Soviet soldiers stormed into the Parliament building after Premier Nagy had just broadcast to the world an agonised call for help.

They marched Mr. Nagy out at gun-point.

He has been charged with supporting counter-revolutionary forces, East Berlin radio said tonight.

IT WAS 2 A.M. when the massacre of Hungary began.

AT 11 A.M. telephone from Budapest to the free world went dead.

AT NOON Moscow announced: 'The Hungarian counter-revolution has been crushed.' . . .

One of the last broadcasts heard from the freedom fighters was a heart-rending call for help.

'Civilised people of the world. On the watch tower of 1,000-year-old Hungary the last flames begin to go out.

The Soviet Army is attempting to crush our troubled hearts. Their tanks and guns are roaring over Hungarian soil.

Our women – mothers and daughters – are sitting in dread. They still have terrible memories of the Army's entry in 1945. Save our souls. S O S – S O S. . . .

Listen to our cry. Start moving. Extend to us brotherly hands. People of the world, save us. S O S. Help, help, help. God be with you and with us.'

Daily Mail, 5 November 1956.

G The return of the Russian troops, 4 November 1956

George Mikes, a Hungarian writer, has lived in England for many years. He returned to Hungary in 1956 to report on the uprising for BBC Television.

The 'outrages in 1945 and . . . 1849' are references to the Russian take-over of Hungary at the end of the Second World War and the crushing of the nationalist revolution of 1848.

The Russian soldiers now arriving in Hungary behaved very differently from their predecessors. **Atrocities** had indeed been committed by the latter, too, but only in exceptional cases. As a rule they had behaved humanely. There was a terrible change in the attitude of the new arrivals. First of all they were angry at having to come at all; most of them had been on the verge of **demobilisation** and they blamed the Hungarian revolution for its postponement. In the second place, they were terrified. There were too many burnt-out Russian tanks to be seen, although these were towed away as soon as possible: the Russians didn't want them to be seen. **Molotov cocktails** had claimed many victims and even when the crew succeeded in jumping out of a burning tank they were, more often than not, shot dead. There were, in the early days at least, a number of AVO agents in their tanks, too, who acted as guides. . . .

The Russians behaved with a savagery which surpassed their outrages in 1945 and even those of 1849. On innumerable occasions they opened fire on bread queues. It only took a single shot to be fired from a building for the huge tanks to stop in front of it and fire until it was razed to the ground.

George Mikes, *The Hungarian Revolution*, André Deutsch, 1957.

H Two views from the British Communist Party

(i) The view of the newspaper of the Communist Party of Great Britain, the *Daily Worker*, now renamed the *Morning Star*.

'Mindszenty' was a Roman Catholic Cardinal who had been imprisoned because of his opposition to the government of Rakosi.

NEW HUNGARIAN ANTI-FASCIST GOVT IN ACTION
Soviet troops called in to stop White Terror

A NEW Workers and Peasants Government was formed in Hungary yesterday led by Janos Kadar, to rescue the country from the new danger of fascism and to safeguard the post-war gains of the people.

It called for Soviet aid to close the Austro-Hungarian border, across which fascist elements had been streaming for several days, and to crush the pro-fascist **clique** around Mindszenty which had gained control in Budapest.

The past few days had witnessed shootings and lynchings of hundreds of Communists and workers. . . .

Messages from other Socialist countries, including Yugoslavia, made clear their full support for the Kadar Government and the Soviet action in aiding it.

By last night Soviet forces appeared to have gained control of Budapest – Moscow Radio announced that order had been restored in Hungary and resistance of a negligible handful overcome with the assistance of the Budapest population. . . .

Moscow Radio said 'All honest Hungarian **patriots** are taking an active part in Budapest as well as in other parts of the country in disarming the mutineers and in overcoming individual nests of resistance of fascist groups.'

Daily Worker, 5 November 1956.

(ii) The view of a journalist sacked by the *Daily Worker*.

I was privileged to see the New Hungary collapse like a house of cards as soon as its people rose to their feet, and I must reserve my passion and enthusiasm for the Communists and non-Communists who fought for liberty, won it – and had it torn from their grasp by foreign intervention. Theirs is the glory, not ours. Yes, we Communists are always right; we know all the answers. We are the leaders; we are making history. But here was history being made in a way that none of us had foreseen. Our **preconceived theories** were shattered overnight. Painful though it may be, if we are really Marxists we must be brave enough to revise our theories.

The *Daily Worker* sent me to Hungary, then suppressed what I wrote. Much of what I wrote was concealed even from my colleagues. Both as a Communist and as a human being I believe it my duty to tell the truth about the Hungarian revolution. I believe this will help bring about the urgently-needed **redemption** and rebirth of the British Communist Party, which for too long has betrayed Socialist principles and driven away some of its finest members by defending the indefensible.

Peter Fryer, *Hungarian Tragedy*, Dennis Dobson, 1956.

I   The Soviet view

The Soviet Foreign Minister, Dimitri Shepilov, speaking at the United Nations General Assembly, 19 November 1956.

The action of the popular masses who, on 23 October, came out in protest against the grave mistakes and errors committed by the former leaders of Hungary, was quite justified. However, **reactionary** fascist elements who were endeavouring to undermine and overthrow the popular democratic order soon tried to turn this healthy movement to their own ends. As early as 23 October, during a demonstration in Budapest, attended by a large number of well-intentioned workers, the leaders of the counter-revolutionary underground brought armed gangs which had been previously assembled out into the open. They provoked mass disturbances in Budapest, which later developed into a rising of anti-popular forces.

Desirous of bringing this rising to an end as quickly as possible, the Hungarian Government requested the Government of the Soviet Union to agree to the use of Soviet military units, stationed in Hungary under the Warsaw Treaty, in helping the Hungarian authorities responsible for maintaining order and tranquility in Budapest. . . .

The Soviet Union could not, of course, refuse to respond to the request of a friendly State for help. In a few days, however, realizing that the continued presence of Soviet military units in Budapest might lead to a further deterioration of the situation, the USSR Government, in agreement with the Hungarian Government, ordered the withdrawal of its troops from the Hungarian capital.

What happened then? After Soviet troops had withdrawn from Budapest, the reactionary forces cast aside their masks and launched a brutal campaign of **reprisal** against the democratic leaders of Hungary, against honest Hungarian patriots. During those dark days for Hungary, the fascists hanged honest patriots from lamp-posts along the streets of Budapest. They broke into hospitals and shot the wounded out of hand. They destroyed factories, and set fire to theatres and museums. . . .

Who was immediately responsible for organizing all these crimes? The workers? The peasants? The intellectuals? No. Those responsible for all these crimes . . . belonged to the remnants of the overthrown classes – rich people impoverished by the Communists, former landowners and rich peasants, persecuted clergymen and the like. . . .

Quoted in Hanak, *Soviet Foreign Policy Since the Death of Stalin.*

Glossary

atrocities evil and cruel acts
clique a small group of closely united people
curfew order requiring everyone to stay indoors
demobilisation return to civilian life
fraternal friendly, brotherly
insurrectionary rebellious
liquidate kill, destroy
Molotov cocktails fire bombs made from bottles filled with petrol
patriots people who love and are prepared to defend their country

Plenipotentiary a person with full power to represent his or her government
preconceived theories already formed ideas and beliefs without all the facts
reactionary someone opposed to the 'truly reforming' communist government
redemption deliverance, saving
reprisal retaliation
subjugating putting under harsh control

Questions

1 Study Source A.
  (a) Explain, using your own knowledge, why Stalin's statue was demolished.
  (b) Explain the usefulness of this kind of source.

2 Read Sources B(i) to (iv) and decide whether the following statements are more likely to be true or false. Give your reasons.
  (i) Only factory workers in Hungary disliked communism in the 1950s.
  (ii) Middle-class people were satisfied with the communist government in Hungary in the 1950s.
  (iii) The supporters of communism were unaware of the dislike many people had for the system.

3 In what ways does Budapest Radio (Source C) give the impression that the people who have risen in rebellion are ·in the wrong?

4 Read Source D.
  (a) What position did Andropov hold in the Soviet Government when he died in 1984?
  (b) Explain the meaning and importance of the phrase 'the Hungarian government immediately repudiates the Warsaw Treaty' in the first paragraph.
  (c) Why did the new Hungarian Government appeal to the UN?

5 Compare Sources E and G. Explain why some Hungarians lynched members of the AVO.

6 Make a list from Source F of words and phrases which show that this extract was written by a journalist and not a historian. Explain the reasons for your selection and explain the advantages and disadvantages of Jeffrey Blyth's choice of words.

7 Explain the references to 1945 in Source F and Source G.

8 Compare Sources F and H(i) and explain the differences between them.

9 Compare Sources H(i) and H(ii). Why did Peter Fryer lose his job? Do you sympathise with him? Give reasons for your answer.

10 Write an imaginary speech in answer to Shepilov's (Source I). Use material that is relevant from other extracts in this section.

Chapter 18 Nigeria: from independence to civil war

From 1967 to 1970 a tragic civil war was fought in Nigeria. Was this an entirely internal problem or had other countries, particularly Britain, any responsibility?

Introduction

One hundred years ago there occurred 'the scramble for Africa'. European countries divided up the continent of Africa into colonies for themselves. The imperial countries drew the frontiers of these colonies as a result of bargains among themselves – they paid no attention to the ethnic differences between the people who actually lived there. One of the largest of these colonies was Nigeria, which Britain came to control. Its population today is about 80 million. And, as you can see from Source A, it contains many different ethnic groups.

In the 1950s Britain was forced to reconsider its colonial policy as more and more colonies demanded independence, but Nigeria did not achieve independence until 1960. This was partly because the north and the south had been ruled separately by the colonial government and it was necessary

A   The main ethnic groups in Nigeria, 1952–53

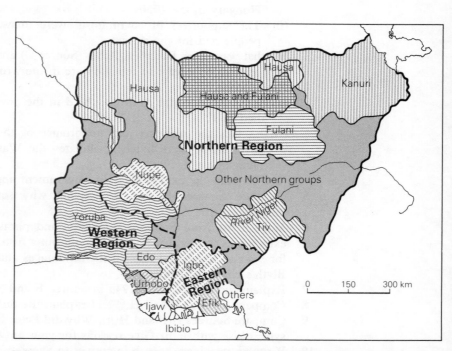

Redrawn from a map in *Conflict in Nigeria: the British View* (Central Office of Information), 1 May 1969.

to unite the two regions under one stable government. The solution was a federal constitution – that is, a certain amount of power was given to three regional governments, Northern, Western and Eastern.

However, the three regions found it impossible to work together and as the situation deteriorated a group of young army officers staged a coup in 1966 and the prime minister was murdered as well as the leaders of the Northern and Western Regions. Gradually the Hausa-Fulani people in the North and the Yoruba in the West became concerned about domination by the Igbo in the East. Quarrels between the Igbo living in the North and the local Hausa-Fulani people became so serious that many people were massacred. The Igbo fled to be with their own people in the Eastern Region, which declared itself independent of the rest of Nigeria under the name of Biafra. The leader of the independence movement was the military commander of the Eastern Region, Colonel Ojukwu. After a long and dreadful civil war (1967–70) Biafra was subdued by the Federal Nigerian army.

B The British Prime Minister meets the Nigerian Prime Minister

Harold Macmillan describes a meeting with Sir Abubakar Tafawa Balewa at the time of independence, 12 January 1960.

The election referred to was in December 1959 in preparation for the formation of an independent government.

[Abubakar] frankly conceded the dangers that lay ahead. . . . He observed to me that 'all the main parties had fought the election on the basis that they had the national interest at heart'. I replied that this was true of most parliamentary elections. Yes, but here there was a difference. Although they made this claim the regional pull was very strong. The Prime Minister added that 'considerable bitterness had been aroused during the election campaign'. He had now to work hard to nurse the country into a sense of national unity. He went on to explain the complications within the regions. Each party, although primarily based on its own region, would try to gain ground in the others by exploiting tribal or religious differences.

Harold Macmillan, *Pointing the Way, 1959–61*, Macmillan, 1972.

C The Nigerian Prime Minister speaking on Independence Day, 1 October 1960

This is a wonderful day, and is all the more wonderful because we have awaited it with increasing impatience, compelled to watch one country after another overtaking us on the road when we had so nearly reached our goal. But now we have acquired our rightful status and I feel sure that history will show that the building of our nation proceeded at the wisest pace: it has been thorough and Nigeria now stands well-built upon firm foundations.

Today's ceremony marks the **culmination** of a process which began fifteen years ago and has now reached a happy and a successful conclusion. . . .

. . . I pay tribute to the manner in which successive British Governments have gradually transferred the burden of responsibility to our shoulders. The assistance and unfailing encouragement which we have received from each Secretary of State for the Colonies and their intense personal interest in our development has immeasurably lightened that burden.

All our friends in the Colonial Office must today be proud of their handiwork and in the knowledge that they have helped to lay the foundations of a lasting friendship between our two nations.

Quoted in A. Burns, *History of Nigeria*, Allen & Unwin, 1969.

D Declaration of Biafran independence

Colonel Ojukwu reads out the declaration, 30 May 1967

Fellow countrymen and women, you, the people of Eastern Nigeria:

Conscious of the supreme authority of Almighty God over all Mankind; of your duty to yourselves and **posterity**;

Aware that you can no longer be protected in your lives and in your property by any government based outside Eastern Nigeria;

Believing that you are born free and have certain **inalienable** rights which can best be preserved by yourselves;

Unwilling to be unfree partners in any association of a political or economic nature;

Rejecting the authority of any person or persons other than the Military Government of Eastern Nigeria to make any imposition of whatever kind or nature upon you;

Determined to dissolve all political and other ties between you and the former Federal Republic of Nigeria;

Prepared to enter into such association, treaty or alliance with any sovereign state within the former Federal Republic of Nigeria and elsewhere on such terms and conditions as best to **subserve** your common good;

Affirming your trust and confidence in me;

Having **mandated** me to proclaim on your behalf and in your name, that Eastern Nigeria be a sovereign independent Republic,

NOW THEREFORE, I LIEUTENANT-COLONEL CHUKWUEMEKA ODUMEGWU OJUKWU, MILITARY GOVERNOR OF EASTERN NIGERIA, BY VIRTUE OF THE AUTHORITY, AND PURSUANT TO THE PRINCIPLES RECORDED ABOVE, DO SOLEMNLY PROCLAIM THAT THE TERRITORY AND REGION KNOWN AS AND CALLED EASTERN NIGERIA, TOGETHER WITH HER CONTINENTAL SHELF AND TERRITORIAL WATERS SHALL HENCEFORTH BE AN INDEPENDENT SOVEREIGN STATE OF THE NAME AND TITLE OF 'THE REPUBLIC OF BIAFRA'.

Quoted in F. Forsyth, *The Making of African Legend: The Biafran Story*, 1969, Penguin ed., 1977.

E The policy of starvation

Frederick Forsyth, who reported the Nigerian Civil War for the *Daily Express* and *Time* magazine before becoming a famous novelist, describes the policy.

It was the starvation in Biafra that really woke up the consciousness of the world to what was going on. The general public, not only of Britain, but of all western Europe and America, though usually unable to **fathom** the political complexities behind the war news, could nevertheless realize the wrong in the picture of a starving child. It was on this image that a press campaign was launched which swept the western world, caused governments to change their policy, and gave Biafra the chance to survive, or at least not to die **unchronicled**.

But even this issue was fogged by propaganda suggesting the Biafrans themselves were 'playing up the issue' and using the hunger of their own people to solicit world sympathy for their political aspirations. There is not one priest, doctor, relief worker or administrator from the dozen European countries who worked in Biafra throughout the last half of 1968 and watched several hundred thousand children die miserably, who could be found to suggest the issue needed any 'playing up'. The facts were there, the pressmen's cameras popped, and the starvation of the children of Biafra became a world scandal.

The graver charge is that the Biafrans, and notably Colonel Ojukwu, used the situation and even prevented its **amelioration** in order to carry support and sympathy.

F. Forsyth, *The Making of an African Legend.*

F A poster distributed by the Biafran Ministry of Information

G Biafra continues to fight

A report from the African correspondent of the *Los Angeles Times*.

There is no sign of collapse in Biafra, no hint of surrender. Yet anyone who knew the area before the war cannot ignore the cruel contrast. . . . Food, of course, is the main problem. . . . Starvation and **kwashiorkor** have been brought somewhat under control, although the suspension of the Red Cross flights has hampered relief efforts, but Biafra has not slipped back to the horror of a year ago, when a few thousand people died of malnutrition every day. The harshness of life strikes an outsider wherever he looks. . . . More significant and depressing, cruelty and meanness have come to Biafran society. Soldiers sometimes evict refugees from camps and seize whatever food has been planted there; or they beat up relief-agency drivers and commandeer their trucks to transport arms. Army deserters use their weapons to waylay relief trucks and steal food. . . .

There is a weariness in Biafra and a deep desire for peace. But in talking with educated Biafrans, visitors find that all the old bitterness, intensity and defiance remain. 'If they are going to kill us,' says a young journalist, 'let them kill us. If they are going to be the lords and we the conquered, let it happen. But we have sacrificed too much to give up Biafra.' The spirit of Biafra, though battered, is still defiant.

Stanley Meisler, article in *Africa Report*, November 1969.

H Britain and arms supplies

(i) The view of the British Prime Minister.
'Lagos' is the capital of Nigeria and 'Calabar' is a coastal town in south-eastern Nigeria, in what was then Biafra.

By the autumn of 1967 the Federal Government, whose expenditure of ammunition was phenomenal, appealed to Britain for arms supplies. This presented us with a problem which was to be with us for over two years. . . .

The demand for arms supplies meant that our Government was bound to lay itself open to attacks from one side or the other and from their respective supporters in Britain. The following note, dictated by me while flying from Lagos to Calabar at a later stage in the war, set out the position as I saw it at the time:

George Thomson, Commonwealth Secretary, sponsored the request. I had some doubts about getting involved in a civil war, as did certain other colleagues, but the arguments were overwhelming. As the traditional supplier, a refusal would have meant not a lurch into neutrality but a hostile act against a fellow Commonwealth country whom we recognized, and whose **integrity** we supported. Moreover, the Russians were in the wings ready to supply everything Nigeria needed but at the price of a growing grip on Nigeria's internal life. There was the problem, too, of British interests in Nigeria. . . .

I spelled out, in particular, the dangers to the 17,000 British citizens resident in Nigeria, many of them in remote communities.

Harold Wilson, *The Labour Government 1964–70*, Weidenfeld & Nicolson and Michael Joseph, 1971.

(ii) British government policy on arms supplies. Part of a pamphlet, in question and answer form, prepared by the British Government.

A **unilateral** suspension of arms supplies by the United Kingdom, however, would be likely to considerably worsen the present situation. While such a decision would not lead to any lessening of the fighting, it would be taken by Colonel Ojukwu as a deliberate act of support for his attempt to break away from Nigeria, and rebel determination to maintain **secession** by force of arms would thus be given added encouragement. Such an attitude by Britain towards Nigeria would be widely resented, while the war would continue. Moreover, by encouraging those who would welcome the break-up of Nigeria on tribal lines, such action could promote divisions in Nigeria and elsewhere in a way which would be a severe set-back to Africa's progress and development. The United Kingdom, which has long fostered African advancement, believes that this cannot be served by tribalism. This view is also shared by African statesmen, the overwhelming majority of whom have consistently declared their support for a solution based on Nigeria's unity.

Central Office of Information, *Conflict in Nigeria: The British View*, HMSO, 1969.

I Critical views about the policies of outsiders

(i) The Soviet view.

It is undeniable that the internal situation in Nigeria would not have led to such devastating consequences had it not been for the fanning of the conflict by the imperialist governments and their support of the separationists in the form of arms and political assistance. . . .

Behind the scenes of the Nigerian war can clearly be seen the **machinations** of the largest oil companies of the world.

Pravda, 13 January 1970. Quoted in *Crisis Paper No. 7: The Nigerian Civil War: the Defeat of Biafra*, Atlantic Information Centre for Teachers, 1970.

(ii) The French view.
  U Thant was Secretary-General of the United Nations at this time.

. . . the extent of the harm might have been considerably reduced if certain great powers had not put their techniques and their armaments at the disposal of the fighting parties. Britain has taken a **hypocritical** attitude all along by supplying arms to Lagos while commiserating with the victims these same arms caused in the other camp. The powers who helped Biafra, including France, cannot be entirely redeemed of the blame of having encouraged underhand traffic of arms in their pursuance of less creditable political and commercial ends. . . .

It is true that the main reason for Biafra's relative isolation in Africa was the fear of almost all the established governments lest the **precedent** of secession led to others in the area. A similar fear explains the almost total inaction of the United Nations and its reluctance to intervene even at the cruellest moments of the conflict, as well as the **unequivocal** condemnation of secession by U Thant.

Le Monde, 14 January 1970, quoted in *Crisis Paper No. 7*.

(iii) A British view opposed to the government.
  'Caritas' is a Roman Catholic charity.

'General Gowon,' says our **complacent** Foreign Secretary, is 'a **magnanimous** man' – and certainly, in the aftermath of the Nigerian civil war, it is important for the British Government to give this impression of the **potentate** they have consistently supported throughout the horror of the past two and a half years. Unfortunately the General's magnanimity is strictly limited by his new circumstances. . . .

When the General characterised the gifts of humanitarians the world over as 'blood money', he was giving the show away. There can only be one reason for him to treat Caritas, Joint Church Aid and the International Red Cross as hostile organisations. It is that their efforts defeated, for a time, his purpose of starving the Biafrans out.

Whether a food blockade is a legitimate weapon of war is a matter for argument, but it is certainly no foundation for peace.

The Sunday Telegraph, 18 January 1970, quoted in *Crisis Paper* No. 7.

Glossary

amelioration improvement
complacent self-satisfied
continental shelf shallow coastal sea-bed
crass stupid
culmination end
fathom understand
hypocritical pretending to be better than it is
inalienable cannot be legally taken away
integrity honesty
kwashiorkor disease resulting from malnutrition

machinations plots
magnanimous generous-hearted
mandated given instructions
posterity all future generations
potentate ruler, monarch
precedent something taken as an example for subsequent events
pursuant to following from
secession breaking away
subserve help
unchronicled not recorded in writing
unequivocal definite and without questioning
unilateral by one country only

Questions

1 Look at the map (Source A) and name the regions where the following ethnic groups mainly live: Hausa-Fulani; Yoruba; Igbo.

2 Compare the views expressed by Sir Abubakar Tafawa Balewa in Sources B and C. How do you explain the differences?

3 Source D is written in legal language. Use this information to write a speech Ojukwu might have made to persuade a meeting of Igbo people that the creation of an independent Biafra was justified.

4 What does Source F tell you about the nature of the fighting in the Nigerian Civil War? What was the purpose of the poster?

5 Read Source E and explain, using your own knowledge also: (a) why starvation occurred in Biafra; (b) why anyone should suggest that the Biafrans were exaggerating the scale of the famine; (c) why Ojukwu might have hindered food supplies to his own people.

6 What evidence is there in Source G that organised military operations by the Biafrans against the federal army were coming to an end by November 1969?

7 Read Sources H(i) and H(ii).
   (a) Make a list of the reasons given by the British Government for continuing to supply arms to the Federal Government of Nigeria after the outbreak of civil war.
   (b) Which argument or arguments do you think most justified the government in pursuing this policy? Give your reasons.

8 Read Sources I(i), (ii) and (iii). Outline in your own words the different points of view in these extracts and explain why the views are different.

Chapter 19 The Caribbean: Commonwealth countries

The former British colonies in the Caribbean (see Source B) are small and poor. One idea put forward to help them was to create a federation.

Introduction

The story of these countries in the twentieth century is very complicated so here we have concentrated on the period around 1960 and on two countries: Jamaica and Trinidad and Tobago.

Many people have settled in the Caribbean over the centuries. The original people were Indians – that is, Amerindians and not to be confused with the Indians who have come from Asia more recently. When the Europeans captured these lands some of them settled – first the Spaniards in the fifteenth and sixteenth centuries, then the British from the seventeenth century. Then, in order to work the plantations, the Europeans brought people from Africa and made them slaves. After the abolition of slavery in 1834 there was again a shortage of people to work on the land. This time people from Asia were shipped to the Caribbean to work as indentured labour (that is, they were contracted to work for three years or more before being free to seek paid employment).

During the nineteenth century the demand for sugar declined and as a result the economies of the Caribbean islands suffered. The early twentieth century saw a further decline and, partly as a result of this situation, support for federation began to grow in the 1930s and 1940s. Labour leaders in the Caribbean believed that a federation would enable the islands to demand a higher price for their goods. However, it was not until 1958 that the Federation came into being and then not all the British colonies joined. After only four years it split up and the various countries became independent, but the problem of poverty remained as a troublesome effect of the colonial period.

A Population pressures

A writer highlights one of the major problems in the West Indies in the 1950s.

In 1957 a Jamaican cartoonist drew a coat of arms for the new West Indian federation. It is a circlet surmounted by two seahorses and bound together by sheaves of sugar cane and by the motto 'For All Togetherness'. Two palm trees on a sandy beach fill the circle, around which are scattered various West Indian fruits and a pair of **machetes**. In the center is a shield, **emblazoned with** a shovel, a rake, and some more fruit – a pineapple, a banana, a coconut. On top of the shield – directly between the machetes – is a baby. After all, the artist explains, 'One of our principal products is babies.'

A great many babies are born in the West Indies: 125,000 each year in a population of three and a quarter million. According to most standards the West Indies are desperately overpopulated: on the average there are 400 people to a square mile, and only half an acre of cultivable land per person. Plantations hold much of the best terrain; only a few of the hundreds of thousands of small farmers own or rent enough land to support their families. For the rest, additional outside work is essential.

David Lowenthal, 'The Social Background of West Indian Federation' in D. Lowenthal (ed.), *The West Indies Federation: Perspectives on a New Nation*, Columbia University Press, 1961.

B   Commonwealth countries in the Caribbean

The map shows the members of the Federation of the West Indies formed in 1958.

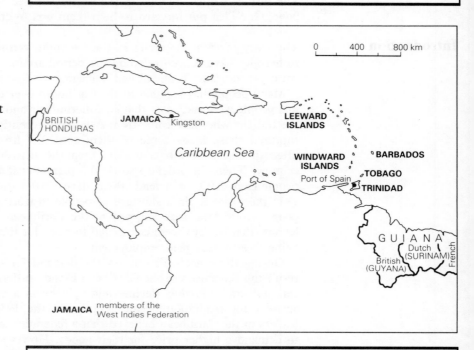

C   Unemployment

Sir Philip Sherlock was Vice-Chancellor of the University of the West Indies (UWI). Here, he is quoting the author of a book about the development of Jamaica since the Second World War.

'West Kingston' is a poor suburb of Kingston, the capital of Jamaica. 'Black Power leaders' were part of a movement demanding better conditions for black people.

Jefferson's remarks about Jamaica hold good for most if not all of the Commonwealth Caribbean:

> Unemployment is undoubtedly Jamaica's gravest problem. Unlike developed countries Jamaica makes no provision for unemployment insurance and the unemployed are forced to rely on the charity of relatives or friends. . . . In addition to the seventeen per cent unemployment rate reported in the Labour Force Survey of 1957, it was brought to light that sixteen per cent of the employed labour force worked for three days or less in the survey week. . . .

A point is reached when the meaning of these figures is written in fire and blood. In October 1966 the Government of Jamaica had to declare a state of emergency in order to check disorder and violence in West Kingston, where the largest number of urban unemployed exist. . . . In the spring of 1970 disorders broke out in Trinidad, one of the most prosperous countries in the Commonwealth Caribbean. The unemployed staged marches and demonstrations, Black Power leaders attacked the Government on the grounds that political independence was meaningless if the black and East Indian masses remained poor while foreign investors made the crucial financial decisions, and a part of the army mutinied.

P. Sherlock, *West Indian Nations: A New History*, Macmillan Jamaican Publishing House, 1973. The quotation from Owen Jefferson is from *The Post-War Development of Jamaica*, Institute of Social and Economic Research, UWI, 1972.

D Poverty and tension

Two writers describe the situation in West Kingston (see Source C), Jamaica, in the early 1970s.

'Rastas' are Rastafarians – members of a Jamaican religion based on the belief that the Emperor of Abyssinia was God.

They're Christian kids from the country, most of them, who hit shantytown with high hopes, and all they found were too many people living in oil drums and fruit-crates and one-room plywood outhouses, with nothing inside except a formica dinette and a glass cabinet for the family china and a radio blasting. West Kingston, literally, is a garbage dump. It used to be a fishing village outside town, and then the city started reclaiming the harbour and they turned it into a dump. Soon, the Israelites appeared – lost tribes of dirt-poor unemployed, homeless scavengers and vagrant Rastas, all washed up there in the rising stench. They built shacks and huts out of cardboard and rusty old iron, and the place spread like a disease till now it's teeming. . . . In the sixties the bulldozers moved in, the builders chased the squatters off Ackee Walk and put up a few concrete highrises, but already they look like they're ready to fall down and bury whole families alive. West Kingston remains a bombsite landscape of live garbage and boxwood and unlikely tropic greenery.

And still they come to town, gangling teenage runaways from the canefields and five-acre farms, all looking for something faster than chopping cane and humping bananas all their lives. . . .

The plantation owners – and for some reason, many of them are Scots – still live in the big houses on top of the hill. The white plantation staff, the overseers and production managers and so on, live in bungalows about half way down. And at the bottom, in a mean straggle of boxwood and corrugated iron, that's where the field workers live.

Adrian Boot and Michael Thomas, *Jamaica: Babylon on a Thin Wire*, Schocken Books, 1977.

E The West Indies Federation

Norman Manley's radio broadcast of 9 June 1960 demanded a referendum in Jamaica on whether to stay in or leave the West Indies Federation. Manley, a highly respected lawyer, was Prime Minister of Jamaica, 1955–62

The West Indies, all these ten islands now united in federation, is a remarkable part of the world. We all have a common history. We all have common problems. Long before federation we were forced to work together in a hundred different ways. We cannot do without each other and whenever we get together we mean more in the world than when we try to stand alone. Each of us alone is small in the world today as size goes in this world of ours. Because we are small it is the simple truth that for us unity is strength and the only hope of strength. . . .

Think of what an independent West Indies will mean in the world when we sit with the other nations in the councils of the United Nations, when our Prime Minister sits as of right with all the other Prime Ministers of the Commonwealth.

Think of what it will mean to Africa and among Africans, what it will mean in the United States where countless thousands of West Indians and their descendants now live. . . .

The greatest issue before mankind after the issue of peace or war is the question of the equality and brotherhood of all the races of mankind on this earth. Made in God's image – black and brown, yellow and white – behold brethren how good a thing it is to dwell together in unity. We, almost alone among all peoples are learning, have nearly learnt how to dwell together in unity.

So the West Indian nation has a manifest duty to go forth as a free people in the world as an example of unity accomplished, of prejudice overcome, of brotherhood realised.

Quoted in R. Nettleford (ed.), *Norman Washington Manley and the New Jamaica*, Longman Caribbean, 1971.

F The problems of federation

A Swiss view of the situation.

Each one of the Commonwealth Caribbean communities . . . lived its own life for centuries, cut off from neighboring communities with which transactions were virtually non-existent, and **oriented** towards the **metropolis**. West Indians had no means and little reason to get to know one another and reach an awareness of what they had in common. . . . The **charismatic** 'heroes' of independence were local 'heroes' who **seduced** the masses by appealing first of all to local sentiment. Nearly every island, nearly every territory had its 'hero' and none of them exercised any form of **pre-eminence** over the Commonwealth Caribbean as a whole. If at the dawn of independence it was possible to speak of a nation . . . it was probably not a West Indian nation, but rather a Jamaican or Trinidadian one. . . .

Did the masses in fact have any opinion on integration? Did they know what it was about? Even more, did they feel a sense of belonging to a West Indian nation? It would seem at first impression that the horizon of the vast majority has continued to be limited to the immediate environment, to a fairly small community. . . . The masses hardly ever travel and have virtually no contact with the inhabitants of other islands. There is very little awareness of what West Indians have in common: a culture, a history, not to speak of a present characterized by a similarity of problems.

Jean F. Freymond, *Political Integration in the Commonwealth Caribbean*, Institut Universitaire de Hautes Etudes Internationales, 1980.

G Norman Manley's Presidential address

He is speaking at the annual conference of the People's National Party (PNP), 16 September 1962.

Comrades, it is one thing to become free; it is another thing to build a real nation of your country (applause). . . .

But, comrades, we start our nationhood with some great assets. One of the good things is the long time that it has taken us to evolve our life into freedom as a people. We have learned much over the last twenty-four years in this country; and we have only got to remember the lessons we have learned to make sure that we can find the right way for the future.

And I dare to claim one other great asset Jamaica has, moving into nationhood, and that is the last seven and a half years of PNP Government in the land. It is not only that we transformed the economy of the country and took her out of the colonial pattern and laid the foundations of a modern State by creating the institutions which a modern State requires in the world by building our resources as fast as we could, by tackling the great problems of the country and the needs of the ordinary people of the country for education and for the human decencies of life. It is not only those things, but it is also that we gave this country for seven and a half years a Government of honesty and integrity. . . .

We have one third great asset in this country, moving into nationhood, and that is the quality of the people of the land, a people tough and resilient, taught by adversity to endure hardship with patience, given some special spirit of loyalty to inspire them in their devotion to the causes they **espoused**, a people well understanding right from wrong, well understanding decency in government, well understanding justice and the rule of law.

Quoted in Nettleford (ed.), *Norman Washington Manley and the New Jamaica*.

H Eric Williams speaking to a children's rally, 1962

Dr Williams is speaking the day before independence in Port-of-Spain, the capital of Trinidad and Tobago. He was Prime Minister from 1962 until his death in 1981.

You, the children, yours is the great responsibility to educate your parents. Teach them to live together in harmony, the difference being not race or colour of skin but merit only, differences of wealth and family status being rejected in favour of equality of opportunity. I call upon all of you young people to practise what you sing today and tomorrow, to translate the ideal of our National Anthem into a code of everyday behaviour, and to make our Nation one in which 'ev'ry creed and race find an equal place'. . . .

. . . On your scholastic development the salvation of the Nation is dependent. At the birth of our Nation, four of its leading personalities, four of the people with the heaviest responsibility for its guidance, in the Cabinet, Parliament and the judiciary, are scholarship winners, educated abroad at the expense of your parents, the taxpayers; the Prime Minister, the Chief Justice, the Deputy Prime Minister and Leader of the House of Representatives, and the Leader of the Opposition. When you return to your classes after Independence, remember therefore, each and every one of you that you carry the future of Trinidad and Tobago in your school bags.

Quoted in Eric Williams, *Inward Hunger*, André Deutsch, 1969.

Glossary

bauxite aluminium ore
charismatic with magnetic personality
emblazoned with showing as heraldic symbols
espoused supported
fiscal taxation
machetes heavy knives, for cutting down sugar cane

metropolis a colony's mother-country, i.e. Britain
nominal in name only
oriented directed
pre-eminence superiority
seduced came to control

Questions

1   Read Source A.
   (a) Draw the cartoon coat of arms.
   (b) Explain the meaning of the symbols and say whether you think that the artist was serious when he drew it.

2   Look at Source B. What difficulty for the Federation does it highlight?

3   What do Sources A and C tell you about problems facing the Caribbean region?

4   Source D describes a particular place. Explain how this illustrates some of the general problems analysed in other extracts in this section.

5   Compare Sources E and F.
   (a) What were the arguments for federation?
   (b) What were the arguments against federation?
   (c) Use the evidence in these extracts to write an imaginary television discussion about the West Indies Federation between Norman Manley and Jean Freymond.

6   Read Source G.
   (a) Why do you think that Manley is giving such an optimistic view of Jamaica's prospects?
   (b) From evidence in other sources in this section explain whether you think that this optimism was justified.

7   Read Source H.
   (a) Why is Dr Williams appealing to the children? What does he expect of them?
   (b) Why does he ask them 'to educate your parents'?

Part 5　Human rights

Chapter 20　Anti-Semitism: the Nazi persecution

One of the most horrific episodes in twentieth-century history was the 'Holocaust' – the massacre of Jews by the Nazis. How could a civilised country like Germany have been responsible for such a crime?

Introduction

In the nineteenth century some scientists came to believe that it was possible to divide mankind into different races. Some even believed that some races were 'better' than others. Adolf Hitler, the man who became dictator of Germany from 1933 to 1945, was very attracted by these theories. He declared that the Aryan or German race was the best and was destined to become the 'Master Race'. He also declared that the purity of this great race was in danger from the Jews.

On the basis of these wild theories the Nazis started a campaign of hatred against the Jews. The campaign turned to violence and, eventually, to the wholesale murder of six million Jewish people.

In order to understand and discuss this topic, you will need to be familiar with a number of words. These are the most important:

race　a human group, all members of which are supposed to have the same physical characteristics
racialism　the belief that some races are superior to others
racism　treating people in a prejudiced way because of their racial difference
anti-Semitism　the word 'Semite' strictly means the racial group living in the Middle East. In practice it has come to mean just Jews. Anti-Semitism is anti-Jewish racism
indoctrination　making people believe something without giving them the opportunity to consider alternatives
genocide　the killing of a whole people or nation

A　Evidence of Edgar Mowrer

He was Berlin correspondent for the *Chicago Daily News* until the Nazis forced him to leave, largely because of what he had written in his book.

The 'Kurfürstendamm' was a street in Berlin.

One spring day in the year 1932, a yellow-haired German maiden was strolling along the Kurfürstendamm in Berlin, when an unshaved, frowsy-looking individual thrust a card into her hand and vanished into the crowd. She glanced at the card, started, grew slightly pale and finally laughed. This is what she read:

'You associate with a Jew.

'It is unworthy of a German woman to pay any attention at all to a Jew – to say nothing of mixing with him. We suppose that you are not aware of the import of your action, and warn you.

'Should it result from our further observations that this warning has no influence upon you, that is, that you continue to be-Jew yourself, then your name will be put down in the register of those women who possessed no pride of race and threw themselves away on a Jew. In a new Germany, a visible sign will be etched or branded on the face of such persons, as a sign for every German man.

'Do not believe that this is a joke or an empty threat. You have been warned and will be further observed.'

This card came into my hands.

When the young lady mentioned the matter to the police she was told that although such cards had frequently been distributed in public places, it had been impossible to trace their origin. It was possible that they originated with persons associated with or friendly to the National-Socialist party. It was also possible that they were the work of some feeble-minded fanatic whose brain had been turned by the anti-semitic campaign that rages throughout contemporary Germany.

Edgar Mowrer, *Germany Puts the Clock Back*, 1933, Penguin ed., 1938.

B   The front page of the newspaper *Der Stürmer*, 1 May 1934

It was published in Nuremberg and was notorious for its vicious attacks on the Jews.

Here are translations of some of the headlines: 'Ritual Murder Number'; 'Jews' Murder Plan against non-Jews Discovered'. The caption under the cartoon reads: 'For thousands of years the Jew has spilt human blood prior to secret rituals. The devil is still stabbing us in the neck today – it is up to you to destroy the devil's breeding-ground'.

C Hitler's views

If we review all the causes which contributed to bring about the downfall of the German people we shall find that the most profound and decisive cause must be attributed to the lack of insight into the racial problem and especially in the failure to recognize the Jewish danger.

It would have been easy enough to endure the defeats suffered on the battlefields in August 1918. They were nothing when compared with the military victories which our nation had achieved. . . .

Nations that make mongrels of their people or allow their people to be turned into mongrels sin against the Will of Providence. . . .

But the loss of racial purity will wreck inner happiness for ever. It degrades men for all time to come. And the physical and moral consequences can never be wiped out.

Adolf Hitler, *Mein Kampf*, 1924, translated by J. Murphy.

D 'Poisonous Fingers'

A short story from a German children's book written in the 1930s.

Inge sits in the reception room of the Jewish doctor. She has to wait a long time . . . she glances through the papers on the table but is too nervous to read: she remembers what her mother has told her and again and again her mind reflects on the warnings of her leader of the League of German Girls. A German girl must not consult a Jew doctor. Many a girl who went to a Jewish doctor to be cured has met with disease and disgrace. Inge has now been waiting for over an hour. Again she picks up the papers in an endeavour to read. Then the door opens. The Jew appears. She screams. In terror she drops the paper. Horrified she jumps up. Her eyes stare into the face of the doctor, and his face is the face of the Devil. In the middle of the Devil's face is a huge crooked nose. Behind the spectacles gleam two criminal eyes. Around the thick lips plays a grin that means, 'Now I have you at last, you little German girl!'

And then the Jew approaches her. His fat fingers clutch at her. But now Inge has got hold of herself. Before the Jew can grab her she smacks his fat face with her hand. One jump to the door. Breathlessly she runs down the stairs and escapes from the Jew's house.

Quoted in Lord Russell, *The Scourge of the Swastika*, Cassell, 1954.

E The Nuremberg Laws

Law of the Protection of German Blood and Honour, 15 September 1935. This was part of the new race regulations generally known as the Nuremberg Laws.

ARTICLE 1. (1) Any marriages between Jews and citizens of German or **kindred** blood are herewith forbidden. Marriages entered into despite this law are invalid, even if they are arranged abroad as a means of **circumventing** this law. . . .

ARTICLE 2. Extramarital relations between Jews and citizens of German or kindred blood are herewith forbidden.

ARTICLE 3. Jews are forbidden to employ as servants in their households female subjects of German or kindred blood who are under the age of 45 years. . . .

ARTICLE 5. (1) Anyone who acts contrary to the prohibition noted in Article 1 renders himself liable to **penal servitude**. (2) The man who acts contrary to the prohibition of Article 2 will be punished by sentence to either a jail or penitentiary.

Quoted in Snyder, *The Idea of Racialism.*

F A model course in modern German history

Part of a course which was recommended in the official teachers' journal in 1934.

'Dawes and Young' were men who drew up plans to reduce the amount of reparations to be paid by Germany after the First World War.

'Schlageter' was executed by the French after the First World War and the Nazis treated him as a hero.

Weeks	Subject	Relations to the Jews
25–28	Adolf Hitler. National Socialism.	Judah's foe!
29–32	The bleeding frontiers. Enslavement of Germany. The Volunteer Corps. Schlageter.	The Jew profits by Germany's misfortunes. Loans (Dawes, Young).
33–36	National Socialism at grips with crime and the underworld.	Jewish instigators of murder. The Jewish press.
37–40	Germany's Youth at the Helm! The Victory of Faith.	The last fight against Judah.

National Socialist Educator, no. 42, 1934, quoted in R. A Brady, *The Spirit and Structure of German Fascism*, Gollancz, 1937.

G Joe de Haas remembers

He was born in Oldenburg in north-west Germany and now lives in England. He wrote this article for the *Guardian* in 1985.

'Kristal Night' was an organised Nazi attack on Jewish homes, shops and synagogues, so-called because many windows were smashed. Joe de Haas's father had the title 'Landes-rabbine', meaning that he was a Jewish religious leader.

Oldenburg has also the 'distinction' of having the first Nazi state government, even before Hitler came to power in Berlin. It is strange to recall, however, that there was very little active anti-semitism, at least until 1938.

The Jews – small shop-keepers, farmers, cattle dealers and breeders – were submerged in the local population both so far as their residences and occupations were concerned.

All this changed with the Kristal Night of the November 9, 1938 when the synagogue was put to the torch, Jewish shops vandalised and the total male Jewish population arrested and put into Sachsenhausen concentration camp. The men were, however, released once they could prove that they had valid immigration papers to enter another country. In the 1930s there were nearly 400 Jews in Oldenburg. Now there are two. Forty per cent of the original numbers perished in one or other of the concentration camps.

My wife and I were in a quandary when we received the mayor's invitation to visit. We spoke to two other former residents of Oldenburg now living in England, who refused to ever set foot into that cursed land. We decided to go, if for no other reason than to visit the grave of my father, Landesrabbiner Dr Philip de Haas who died in Oldenburg in 1935. . . .

Joe de Haas, 'Forgiving Without Forgetting', *Guardian*, 26 June 1985.

Glossary

circumventing avoiding
kindred related
mastication chewing

penal servitude imprisonment with
hard labour

Questions

1 What evidence is there in Source A that anti-Semitism was rife in Germany before Hitler came to power?

2 It is sometimes said, 'If it is in the newspaper, it must be true'. How would you reply to someone who said this about Source B?

3 Read Source C.
(a) Why does Hitler refer to the First World War?
(b) What does he mean by the word 'mongrel'?

4 Read Sources D and F.
(a) What kind of effects might these sources have had on young people in Hitler's Germany?
(b) How can they be seen as forms of propaganda?

5 What evidence is there in the rest of this chapter to indicate that the law in Source E might not have been entirely unexpected?

6 Read Source G.
(a) Explain the usefulness of this kind of personal evidence.
(b) Explain why historians might question its reliability.
Support your answers by particular reference to this extract.

Chapter 21 South Africa: apartheid

The concept of 'apartheid' was created by the National Party in South Africa and exists only in South Africa. By the 1980s it was condemned throughout the world. Why was it thought to be so objectionable?

Introduction

South Africa is a country made up of several different races. Much of the history of South Africa since 1948 has been about the relations between these different races who have come to South Africa as a result of immigration over the centuries. By far the largest group in South Africa is the Bantu (about 70 per cent of the population). They originated in West Africa before moving to other parts of Africa possibly as long ago as 2000 years. The next largest group is white people whose Dutch ancestors settled there in the seventeenth century and other white people whose British ancestors settled there in the nineteenth century. There is a small group of Asians whose families originally came from India, China or Malaya. Other people are of mixed race, or 'Coloured' as the government calls them, whatever the colour of their skin.

Since 1948 South Africa has been governed by the National Party. This is the party of the Afrikaners, the Dutch white immigrants, whose language is Afrikaans. They have followed a policy of 'apartheid', which is an Afrikaans word meaning 'separateness'. Apartheid is designed to prevent, as far as possible, black and white people from mixing. It has taken two forms. One is called 'petty' apartheid: this is an attempt to separate whites and blacks even when they use the same buildings or services. The other is called 'grand' apartheid: this is an attempt to make black people live in special 'Bantustan homelands', which the government claims can become independent countries.

There is no space here to deal with all the awful aspects of apartheid. The sources mainly try to show what the government has intended and the effect on the lives of those who have been discriminated against.

A 'Crisis in World Conscience'

The title of a speech by Dr H. F. Verwoerd, Prime Minister of South Africa, 3 September 1963. This is an extract from the speech, quoted by official government sources.

No other nation would appear to have a race relations problem as complicated and of such **magnitude** as the one with which we have to cope.

It is our aim to survive and to prosper as a White nation, but we know that this cannot be done by suppressing those entrusted to our care; neither can they be denied the opportunity to develop fully. . . .

If the word *apartheid* was chosen with any aim at all – then it was done to say, both to the Whites and the Blacks and indeed to the whole world, that we do *not* seek to oppress; we do not seek separation in our interests alone. We wish to separate the races so that each individual can enjoy all rights and opportunities among his own people, and where possible, in his own territory. Its objective is friendly, born out of goodwill. Yet the outside world, and even those we call our friends, are not prepared to accept this clear definition of 'apartheid'. They go out of their way – every time they use abusive language against us – to say **dogmatically** apartheid is oppression, born out of race hatred.

Extract from a speech by Dr H. F. Verwoerd, quoted in *Fact Paper 107*, South African Department of Information, 1963.

B   An extract from the *South Africa Yearbook*, 1963

This is published for the South African Government.

1   In one respect South Africa's policy differs radically from that in the rest of Africa. South Africa has never been exclusively a Black man's country. The Bantu have no greater claim to it than its white population. Bantu tribes from Central and East Africa invaded South Africa at the time when Europeans landed at the Cape. . . .

2   The areas chosen by Bantu 300 years ago are still in Bantu hands. . . .

6   It is well nigh impossible to create one nation out of the different population groups inhabiting the Republic of South Africa. Each group clings to its own culture, language and traditions. This natural trend must be respected.

South African Yearbook, South African Department of Information, 1963.

C   Being 'Coloured' in South Africa

Part of the *Report of the United Nations Special Committee on the Policies of 'Apartheid' of the Government of the Republic of South Africa*, 26 October 1967.

In February 1966, Sandra Laing, an eleven-year-old school girl was reclassified 'Coloured' after complaints from some parents in the white boarding school she was attending, despite the fact that her parents and two brothers and a sister were white. She was reported to be a genetic 'throwback' showing certain African features. Shortly after, she was brought home by the school principal and a policeman who told her parents that she could no longer stay in school. In fact, under the *apartheid* laws, she could not even remain with her family unless she was registered as a servant. The father, a storeowner near Piet Retief, reported that his wife was so distressed that she 'often threatened to take her life and to take our daughter with her'. The case was reported in the world press and the family received letters from several countries offering to provide a home for the girl. The father appealed against the classification and indicated that if the judgement was unfavourable, he would seriously consider accepting offers from abroad. On 2 May 1967, the Pretoria Supreme Court dismissed the appeal but suggested that consideration be given to reclassification under the Population Registration Amendment Act of 1967. Subsequently, in July 1967, Sandra Laing was reclassified white, but it was reported that white schools and even convents had declined to admit her.

Quoted in *The Anatomy of Apartheid*, Office of Public Information, United Nations, 1968.

D   Examples of so-called 'petty apartheid'

These examples were quoted in a local South African newspaper.

In no other year since the present Government came into power in 1948 have so many *apartheid* notices been put up, or has so much money been spent on separate entrances, toilets, seating arrangements and other trappings of *apartheid*.

Following are some of the many 'pinpricks' that have been reported, and which have evoked considerable comment this year:

The granting of Government permission for Coloured people to watch rugby at Newlands B field on condition that a 6-foot wire fence is built between them and the White spectators.

The intrusion of four detectives at a symphony concert in the Cape Town City Hall to take the names of a handful of Coloured music-lovers in the audience.

The refusal of permission for White judges to officiate at a Coloured beauty contest in Paarl.

The considerable inconvenience caused to a blind White girl accompanied by a Coloured maid after she had been told by a White taximan in Cape Town that he could not carry White and Coloured passengers in the same car.

The Cape Times, 15 October 1965, quoted in E. Brookes, *Apartheid*, Routledge & Kegan Paul, 1968.

E   A railway station in South Africa

This photograph shows 'petty apartheid' at the railway station.

F The land and the people

The map shows the population of South Africa and the Bantustans.

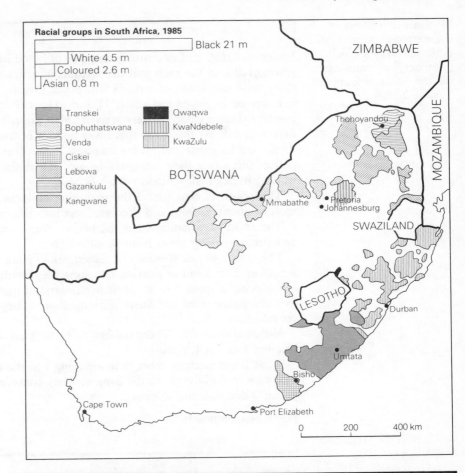

Racial groups in South Africa, 1985

- Black 21 m
- White 4.5 m
- Coloured 2.6 m
- Asian 0.8 m

- Transkei
- Bophuthatswana
- Venda
- Ciskei
- Lebowa
- Gazankulu
- Kangwane
- Qwaqwa
- KwaNdebele
- KwaZulu

G The Soweto demonstrations, June 1976

Soweto is the second largest town in South Africa, built for black people so that they can go to work in Johannesburg, an all-white city 30 kilometres away.

'Sharpeville' was the scene of an infamous incident when police opened fire on unarmed black demonstrators in 1960.

(i) The reasons for the demonstrations.

Protests against the teaching of Afrikaans in schools had been smouldering in Soweto for several weeks before Wednesday's riot. . . . Earlier last week, Councillor Leonard Mosala, of the Soweto Urban Council, warned that teaching through the **medium** of Afrikaans could result in another Sharpeville.

His prophecy came true at 9.30 a.m. on Wednesday. A small group of police tried to stop a protest march of between four and five thousand black schoolchildren. . . .

For Mr John Vorster's Government there could be no question of yielding on this issue: To allow Africans to be educated only in English would be to perpetuate the old relationship whereby the great majority of literate blacks would never learn to speak Afrikaans.

Besides, it would be **tantamount** to acknowledging the hostility of blacks to Afrikaners – and this no Afrikaner-dominated Government could dream of doing.

Colin Legum and David Barritt, 'How Soweto exploded and why it was inevitable', in *The Observer*, 20 June 1976.

(ii) An eye-witness at the demonstrations. Alf Khumalo was a black photographer working for the Johannesburg *Sunday Times*.

Violence. Small bodies writhing in pools of blood in the dust. Police bullets tearing holes in the mob and the screams of anger and pain. These are my most vivid memories of a day I will never forget.

I arrived in Soweto at about 11 a.m. The children were marching with banners. Police troop carriers arrived. Men poured out of the vehicles and fired tear gas. At this stage there was no hint of trouble to come. The children were laughing and joking amongst themselves. They advanced on the police, but when they saw guns being held at the ready they turned and walked back to the Orlando West School.

The police circled round the marching children, who had swelled to a mob of about 12,000, and fired tear gas into the crowd.

The children began stoning the police. Some surrounded the policemen and began stoning them from all directions.

The police began shooting. I remember looking at the children in their school uniforms and wondering how long they would stand up to the police.

Suddenly a small boy dropped to the ground next to me. I realised then that the police were not firing warning shots. They were shooting into the crowd.

More children fell. There seemed to be no plan. The police were merely blasting away at the mob.

What frightened me more than anything was the attitude of the children. Many seemed oblivious to the danger. They continued running towards the police – dodging and ducking.

The Observer, 20 June 1976.

H Bishop Tutu

The Nobel peace prize is an international prize awarded in Sweden to the person considered to have done most in the year for the cause of peace.

Father Huddleston is an English priest who has worked for many years in South Africa.

Bishop Desmond Tutu, the 53-year-old General-Secretary of the South African Council of Churches, who yesterday won the Nobel peace prize, sees himself as a 'simple pastor passionately concerned for justice, peace and reconciliation'. . . .

Bishop Tutu's earnest pleading for justice and **reconciliation** in South Africa drew him into the political arena, although he has always insisted that his motivation is religious, not political. . . .

Bishop Tutu has been attacked by the Conservatives for advocating the intensification of all forms of non-violent pressures against South Africa's **establishment** because, to him, increased pressure is the only alternative to violence. He is not interested in **ameliorative steps** which 'make apartheid bearable rather than dismantle it'. . . .

Bishop Tutu remembers being amazed as a young boy when the then Father Huddleston doffed his hat to his mother, a domestic servant. Father Huddleston, said Bishop Tutu, was the first white man to show that **elementary courtesy**.

It helps account for his warm attitude to whites and his belief that they, too, need 'liberating' from apartheid.

As he told Mr Justice Eloff: 'Oppression dehumanises the oppressor as much as, if not more than, the oppressed . . . whites need to hear and know that their value as persons is **intrinsic** to who they are by virtue of having been created in God's image.'

Patrick Laurence, 'Bishop Tutu's path to peace prize', *Guardian*, 17 October 1984.

Glossary

ameliorative steps gradual reforms
dogmatically without the slightest query
elementary courtesy basic good manners
establishment the people who effectively control the country

intrinsic essential
magnitude great size
medium method of giving information
reconciliation making people friendly towards each other
tantamount the same as

Questions

1 Read Sources A and B.
   (a) Make a list in your own words of the reasons Dr Verwoerd gives in favour of apartheid in Source A.
   (b) Why do you think Verwoerd made this speech?
2 How does Source B reinforce the policy of apartheid?
3 Read Source C. Imagine you were Sandra Laing.
   (a) Write an entry in your diary explaining how you felt when you were re-classified. (Also make use of Sources D and E.)
   (b) Explain why the South African Government has considered race classification to be necessary.
4 (a) The episodes described in Sources D and E were called 'petty apartheid' by the *Cape Times*. Why?
   (b) Write a short speech attacking the system.
5 From the evidence in Source F calculate the percentage of the South African population that is (a) black; (b) white. What does the map tell us about the Bantustans?
6 Read Sources G(i) and (ii). Imagine that you participated in the Soweto demonstration and were arrested. Write out the speech you would make in your own defence.
7 Read Source H. Why do you think Bishop Tutu won the Nobel Peace Prize?
8 (a) List all the newspapers which have been used as sources in this section.
   (b) How important do you think (i) English and (ii) South African newspapers have been in arousing opposition to apartheid?
9 Read Sources A and B again and list the arguments *against* each point made in favour of apartheid.

Chapter 22 The USA: civil rights for black people

Black Americans have had equal rights in law since 1866 but it was not until the 1960s that major attempts were made to improve the conditions and rights of black people in the USA. Why was such a campaign necessary, a hundred years after the abolition of slavery?

Introduction

Until the Civil War of 1861–65 most black Americans were slaves. As a result of that war slavery was abolished; and in 1866 the fourteenth amendment to the US Constitution declared that all American citizens had equal rights and privileges. And yet for at least another century the negroes, as they were called, continued to suffer not just lack of rights and humiliation, but even death, at the hands of white people who were prejudiced to the point of bitter hatred.

Most of the blacks lived in the southern states. There, white people thought up many ways to keep the negroes 'second-class citizens'. Particularly common was 'segregation'. This means keeping white and black people apart by having for example separate schools, separate seats on buses and separate sections in restaurants. And, of course, the services provided for the blacks, especially the schools, were not as good as those provided for the whites. Furthermore, it was made difficult for negroes to vote. For instance, there were complicated registration processes. The blacks found these difficult because of their lack of education, which in turn was the result of bad schools.

However, by the 1950s and 1960s more and more blacks were demanding that they should have equal treatment with whites – that the educational and political barriers to their civil rights should be swept away. (Civil rights are rights which people should have in law by virtue of being a citizen, for example, education, voting, fair trial.) Several US presidents recognised the justice of their cause and introduced reforms.

A The need for self-respect

Stokely Carmichael was a leading member of the protest organisation called 'Black Power'.

Black people must redefine themselves, and only *they* can do that. Throughout this country, vast segments of the black communities are beginning to recognise the need to assert their own definitions, to reclaim their history, their culture; to create their own sense of community and togetherness. There is a growing resentment of the word 'Negro', for example, because this term is the invention of our oppressor; it is *his* image of us that he describes. Many blacks are now calling themselves African-Americans, Afro-Americans or black people because that is *our* image of ourselves. When we begin to define our own image, the **stereotypes** – that is, lies – that our oppressor has developed will begin in the white community and end there. The black community will have a positive image of itself that *it* has created. This means we will no longer call ourselves lazy, apathetic, dumb, good-timers, shiftless, etc. Those are words used by white America to define us. If we accept these adjectives, as some of us have in the past, then we see ourselves only in a negative way, precisely the way white America wants us to see ourselves. Our incentive is broken and our will to fight is surrendered. From now on we shall view ourselves as African-Americans and as black people who are in fact energetic, determined, intelligent, beautiful and peace-loving.

S. Carmichael and C. V. Hamilton, *Black Power: The Politics of Liberation in America*, Jonathan Cape, 1967.

B Schools for blacks

The Civil War amendments were Amendments 13, 14 and 15 to the US constitution, which abolished slavery and gave black Americans rights of citizenship. They were passed between 1865 and 1870.

. . . although there is some sort and some amount of Negro education everywhere, Negro education still does not have a fixed, legitimate, acknowledged place. It is realized that something must be done in order to keep the Negro satisfied and in order to uphold the Americans' slogan of free schools for every child, but it is rare that a community has any real interest in planning or building a wise system of education for the race. Politically, it is not generally admitted that the Negro has a right to schools or to other public services. . . . The Negro is still not recognized as a citizen despite the Civil War amendments.

Bertram Schrieke, *Alien Americans*, 1936, quoted in Gunnar Myrdal, *An American Dilemma*, Harper & Row, 1962 ed.

C The desegregation of schools

(i) The US Supreme Court decision on segregation in education in the case of *Brown* v. *Board of Education, Topeka*, 1954.

In these days, it is doubtful that any child may reasonably be expected to succeed in life if he is denied the opportunity of an education. Such an opportunity, where the state has undertaken to provide it, is a right which must be made available to all on equal terms. . . .

We come then to the question presented: Does segregation of children in public schools solely on the basis of race, even though the physical facilities and other **'tangible' factors** may be equal, deprive the children of the minority group of equal educational opportunities? We believe that it does. . . .

We conclude that in the field of public education the doctrine of 'separate but equal' has no place. Separate educational facilities are inherently unequal. Therefore, we hold that the plaintiffs and others similarly situated for whom the actions have been brought are, by reason of the segregation complained of, deprived of the equal protection of the laws guaranteed by the Fourteenth Amendment.

Quoted in L. L. Snyder, *The Idea of Racialism*, Van Nostrand, 1962.

(ii) A statement presented by Senator Sam T. Ervin Jr. to the North Carolina Senate and House of Representatives, 12 March 1956.

We regard the decision of the Supreme Court in the school cases as a clear abuse of judicial power. . . .

The original Constitution does not mention education. Neither does the Fourteenth Amendment nor any other Amendment. The debates preceding the submission of the Fourteenth Amendment clearly show that there was no intent that it should affect the systems of education maintained by the States. . . .

This unwarranted exercise of power by the Court, contrary to the Constitution, is creating chaos and confusion in the States principally affected. It is destroying the amicable relations between the white and Negro races that have been created through ninety years of patient effort by the good people of both races. It has planted hatred and suspicion where there has been heretofore friendship and understanding. . . .

We commend the motives of those States which have declared the intention to resist forced integration by any lawful means.

Quoted in B. Ziegler (ed.), *Desegregation and the Supreme Court*, D. C. Heath, 1958.

D   The Ku Klux Klan

A letter from J.B. Stoner, 'Imperial Wizard' of the Christian Knights of the Ku Klux Klan, to the New York Police Commissioner, 6 August 1959.

The 'Ku Klux Klan' is a white organisation which originated in the southern states of the USA to terrorise black people. They wear white pointed hoods and robes.

'Harlem' is a poor district of New York with a mainly black population.

Police Commissioner Kennedy, my dear friend, I now offer you the service of the Christian Knights of the Ku Klux Klan for the purpose of maintaining White Supremacy in New York City and for keeping New York niggers in their place. I think 5,000 Klansmen could clean up Harlem for you if you would give them police badges and N.Y. police uniforms to wear instead of their Klan uniforms. They will leave their Klan robes at home so the New York niggers won't know that your police reinforcement are White Christian Klansmen. You can use our Christian Knights as guards to protect every White business in Harlem and also in other New York areas where nigger customers are giving trouble to white business men. After all, how do the black jig-a-boos expect to live without White business to sell them what they need? You can also use our Klansmen to escort White salesmen into Harlem and other parts of New York City that are suffering from the black plague.

Quoted in E. U. Essien-Udom, *Black Nationalism: The Rise of the Black Muslims in the USA*, University of Chicago Press, 1962, Penguin ed. 1966.

E   A speech by Martin Luther King

On 20 August 1963 a quarter of a million people held a demonstration in Washington to support civil rights for black people. They heard one of the most famous speeches on the subject.

I say to you today even though we face the difficulties of today and tomorrow, I still have a dream. It is a dream that is deeply rooted in the American dream. I have a dream that one day this nation will rise up and live out the true meaning of its creed: 'We hold these truths to be self-evident, that all men are created equal.'

I have a dream that one day on the red hills of Georgia the sons of former slaves and the sons of former slave-owners will be able to sit down together at the table of brotherhood. I have a dream that one day even the state of Mississippi will be transformed into an oasis of freedom and justice.

I have a dream that my four little children one day will live in a nation where they will not be judged by the colour of their skin, but by the content of their character.

This will be the day when all of God's children will be able to sing with new meaning 'Let Freedom Ring'. So let freedom ring from the prodigious hilltops of New Hampshire, let freedom ring from the mighty mountains of New York. But not only that. Let freedom ring from every hill and molehill of Mississippi, from every mountainside. When we allow freedom to ring from every town and every hamlet, from every state and every city, we will be able to speed up that day when all God's children, black men and white men, Jews and Gentiles, Protestants and Catholics, will be able to join hands and sing in the words of the old Negro spiritual, 'Free at last! Free at last! Great God Almighty, we are free at last!'

Quoted in Patricia Baker, *Martin Luther King*, Wayland, 1974.

F Conversation between young blacks about the rioting in Detroit, August 1967

The young blacks' word for white people is 'honkies'. Watts, Newark and Harlem are other towns and districts in the USA where blacks rioted in 'the long hot summers', 1964–67.

'Those buildings goin' up was a pretty sight,' a long-legged kid said. 'I sat right here and watched them go. And there wasn't nothin' them honkies could do but sweat and strain to put it out.'

'Yeah, man,' a pal chimed in, 'it's about time those honkies started earnin' their money in this neighborhood.'

'You know,' said Long-Legs, 'we made big news. They called this the country's worst race riot in history.'

'Yeah,' said another gangly kid, straddling the railing. 'My kids goin' to study about that in school, and they'll know their old man was part of it.'

'We got the record man,' exulted another youth. . . . 'They can forget all about Watts and Newark and Harlem. This is where the riot to end all riots was held.'

'The Hard-Core Ghetto Mood' in *Newsweek*, vol. lxx, no. 8, 1967, quoted in Young, *Roots of Rebellion*.

G Television address to the nation by President Kennedy, 11 June 1963

It ought to be possible for American consumers of any color to receive equal service in places of public accommodation, such as hotels and restaurants and theaters and retail stores, without being forced to resort to demonstrations in the street, and it ought to be possible for American citizens of any color to register and to vote in a free election without interference or fear of **reprisal**. . . .

It is better to settle these matters in the courts than on the streets, and new laws are needed at every level, but the law alone cannot make men see right. . . .

Next week I shall ask the Congress of the United States to act, to make a commitment it has not fully made in this century to the proposition that race has no place in American life or law.

Quoted in E. D. Cronon (ed.), *Twentieth Century America*, vol. 2, Dorsey Press, 1966.

H Address by President Johnson to a Joint Session of Congress, 15 March 1965

Many of the issues of civil rights are complex and difficult. But about this there can be no argument. Every American citizen must have an equal right to vote. There is no reason which can excuse the denial of that right. There is no duty which weighs more heavily on us than the duty to ensure that right.

Yet the harsh fact is that in many places in this country men and women are kept from voting because they are Negroes. Every device of which human ingenuity is capable has been raised to deny this right. The Negro citizen may go to register only to be told that the day is wrong, the hour is late, or the official in charge is absent.

If he persists, and manages to present himself to the registrar, he may be disqualified because he cannot spell out his middle name or because he abbreviated a word on the application.

If he manages to fill out an application he is given a test. The registrar is the sole judge of whether he passes this test. He may be asked to recite the entire Constitution, or explain the most complex provisions of state law. Even a college degree cannot be used to prove that he can read or write. For the fact is that the only way to pass these barriers is to show a white skin. . . .

Wednesday I will send to Congress a law designed to eliminate illegal barriers to the right to vote. This Bill will strike down restrictions to voting in all elections – Federal, state, and local – which have been used to deny Negroes the right to vote.

Quoted in United States Information Service, *We Shall Overcome*, 1965.

Glossary

formulation creation
reprisal retaliation
stereotypes the act of stereotyping is to describe a people (a nation or race) by certain characteristics and then assume that all individuals belonging to the group have these characteristics
'tangible' factors things which can be clearly judged, for example, here textbooks and equipment

Questions

1 Read Source A. Explain why words which 'label' people are important.

2 Read Sources B, C(i) and C(ii) and write an imaginary letter by a black person to a newspaper in 1957 explaining the importance and difficulty of obtaining good education for black children.

3 Compare Sources C(i) and (ii). Explain how and why they are different in the attitudes they express.

4 Read Source D. What was the attitude of the writer to blacks?

5 Read Source E. What does Martin Luther King mean by 'freedom' in this extract?

6 What does Source F tell you about the attitude of young blacks to the urban riots of the 'long hot summers' in the 1960s?

7 Read Sources G and H, and with the help of your own knowledge also, decide with which of the following statements you agree. Explain the reasons for your decision.

  (i) Kennedy solved the problem of segregation of blacks but not that of their right to vote.

  (ii) Both Kennedy and Johnson were led to take action for fear of outbreaks of violence.

  (iii) Kennedy believed that a change in the law would have little effect.

  (iv) Johnson was interfering in the rights of the individual states.

8 Look at all the sources in this chapter and, using evidence in the sources and information about the sources, particularly dates, say who you think did most to achieve civil rights for black people: (i) the government or (ii) black people themselves.

Chapter 23 The Middle East: the Palestinians

The Palestinian Arab people and the Israelis have been enemies ever since the creation of Israel in 1948 and especially since the Six-Day War. Why has it been so difficult to find a solution to the Palestinian problem?

Introduction

'Palestine' was a name given to the Holy Land of biblical times. Then, after the First World War, a new Palestine was created from the old Turkish Empire and governed by Britain. Britain had no real right to the land, but two other peoples had. These were the Arab people who had lived there for many centuries; and the Jews, who had lived there in ancient times. The Jews' fight to re-establish themselves in the Holy Land was called Zionism and the Jews who fought for it were known as Zionists. One of the great tragedies of modern history has been the failure of anyone to solve these rival claims.

In 1947 the United Nations took over responsibility for Palestine and arranged for the creation of a Jewish state of Israel there. In 1948 Israel came into being. After a war with its Arab neighbours Israel controlled almost the whole of Palestine. Many of the Palestinian Arab people fled from their homes and became refugees. As a result, they came to live in four main places (see. Source B):

1 Israel,
2 the West Bank of the Jordan (the inhabitants of that region plus refugees),
3 refugee camps in the Gaza Strip,
4 other Arab countries (as refugees).

Wherever they lived the Palestinians dreamed of having a country of their own again. The problem was: how was this to be brought about? Some Palestinians have wanted to abolish Israel as a Jewish state. Others have been willing to accept the idea of a Palestinian 'mini-state' made up of Gaza and the West Bank. Sometimes the leaders have been willing to negotiate. At other times they have used terrorist methods to try to force the rest of the world to take notice of their plight.

The Palestinians have formed several groups to campaign for their cause. Most belong to the Palestine Liberation Organisation (PLO). The PLO operated mainly from Jordan, 1964–70, Lebanon 1970–82, and Tunisia, since 1982. In the 1960s and 1970s one of the most famous groups was 'Black September'. They organised several notorious acts of terrorism, for example, hijacking air-liners. The purpose of terrorism is to gain publicity. But often innocent people are killed.

A   Oath chanted by Palestinian children at the start of the school day

Palestine is our country,
Our aim is to return
Death does not frighten us,
Palestine is ours,
We shall never forget her.
Another homeland we shall never accept!
Our Palestine, witness, O God and History
We Promise to shed our blood for you!

Quoted in D. Hirst, *The Gun and the Olive Branch*, Faber, 1977.

B   The dispersal of the Palestinians

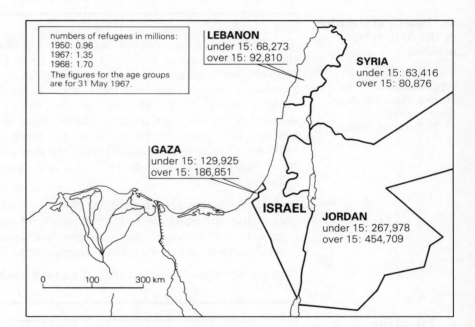

numbers of refugees in millions:
1950: 0.96
1967: 1.35
1968: 1.70
The figures for the age groups
are for 31 May 1967.

LEBANON
under 15: 68,273
over 15: 92,810

SYRIA
under 15: 63,416
over 15: 80,876

GAZA
under 15: 129,925
over 15: 186,851

ISRAEL

JORDAN
under 15: 267,978
over 15: 454,709

0   100   300 km

C   The experience of one refugee

A refugee describes to a French journalist what happened to her and her family.

At that time (1948) we lived near Ramallah. We were a peasant family, and the land belonged to us and we cultivated it ourselves. We also owned some cattle. Then they attacked us and we had to flee. We spent the night, I remember, in a cave in the mountains. And after a long walk, we were eventually put in an UNRWA refugee camp at Ramallah. After a long time we found work, very poorly paid, but it enabled us to eat and we lived, thank the Lord, and just as we were beginning to earn a little more and the family was becoming healthy and happy all of a sudden we heard that there they were again, they had come back to take everything away from us, and we were left with nothing but sandals on our feet and a veil over our heads and practically nothing else, and we were on the road for three days.

We arrived in Amman as street beggars, we knocked at people's doors, and my children, I have eight, were hungry and the babies fell ill with stomach parasites, and they slept on the ground with no covering except a shawl. Then they sent us to a camp at Gerash and gave us bread, just throwing it at us, so it was good luck to them that caught it, and the devil take the rest. After a few days we got flour and were able to bake bread ourselves. All we had to eat was that flour, and we made a paste and gave it to the children with water. One day, after about two months, the winter came, all of a sudden, with torrential rain and even snow, and it all came through into the tent and one of my children, the youngest, died of cold in the snow and the mud.

Quoted in G. Chaliand, *The Palestinian Resistance*, Penguin, 1972.

D Israel's explanation of the Arab refugee problem

The chief Israeli representative at the United Nations, Abba Eban, speaking on 17 November 1958.

The Arab refugee problem was caused by a war of aggression, launched by the Arab States against Israel in 1947 and 1948. Let there be no mistake. If there had been no war against Israel, with its consequent harvest of bloodshed, misery, panic and flight, there would be no problem of Arab refugees today. . . . Caught up in the havoc and tension of war; demoralized by the flight of their leaders; urged on by irresponsible promises that they would return to inherit the spoils of Israel's destruction – hundreds of thousands of Arabs sought the shelter of Arab lands. A survey by an international body in 1957 described these violent events in the following terms:

'As early as the first months of 1948 the Arab League issued orders **exhorting** the people to seek a temporary refuge in neighbouring countries, later to return to their **abodes** in the wake of the victorious Arab armies and obtain their share of abandoned Jewish property.'

Quoted in W. Laqueur (ed.), *The Arab-Israeli Reader*, Weidenfeld & Nicolson, 1969.

E Palestinian terrorism

(i) The views of a British scholar.
  'Neo-Marxist Palestinian factions' are political groups of Palestinians who believe in a modernised form of the Communist teachings of Karl Marx.

It is by no means clear how the wave of Palestinian terrorist attacks on Western airlines, and random slaughter of civilians, is supposed to have assisted their cause. Western opinion was already well aware of the highly charged nature of the Arab–Israel conflict. . . . The main impact on international opinion, even on moderate Arab opinion, was revulsion at attacks on the innocent. As Arab leaders became increasingly aware of the fanaticism of the extreme neo-Marxist Palestinian factions that were mainly involved in promoting terrorism they became increasingly apprehensive about assisting the birth of [a] new militant revolutionary state in their own backyard. . . .

Terrorist attacks on Israel, and on Israeli citizens abroad, have only served to toughen Israeli resistance and political will.

P. Wilkinson, *Terrorism and the Liberal State*, Macmillan, 1972.

(ii) The assassination of Israeli athletes at the Munich Olympic Games. Newspaper comment by a British expert on terrorism.

'Al Fatah' is a terrorist group of the PLO.

[In 1972] the 'Black September' group of Al Fatah . . . seized and killed 11 Israeli athletes at the Munich Olympics. World opinion – already outraged by the massacre of 28 passengers at Lod Airport by Japanese terrorists acting for the PFLP [Popular Front for the Liberation of Palestine] – was intensely hostile. . . .

. . . Moreover, though they have attracted massive publicity they have established the world image of the Palestinian as a terrorist. Their supreme tragedy is that they have killed many more Arabs than Israelis.

Major-General Richard Clutterbuck in the *Guardian*, 24 March 1982.

(iii) The assassination of Israeli athletes at the Munich Olympic Games. Newspaper comment by a Palestinian.

A bomb in the White House, a mine in the Vatican, the death of Mao Tse-tung, an earthquake in Paris could not have echoed through the consciousness of every man in the world like the operation at Munich. . . . It was like painting the name of Palestine on the top of a mountain that can be seen from the four corners of the earth.

Al-Sayyad, 13 September 1972, quoted in Hirst, *The Gun and the Olive Branch*.

F   The determination of Yasser Arafat, leader of the PLO

Beirut, where Yasser Arafat's forces were based in 1984, is the capital of Lebanon.

A delegation of leaders and notables representing the whole Muslim community came to see me [in Beirut]. They came to plead with me to give up the fighting because, they said, the PLO's position was hopeless and there was no point in causing more casualties.

They said to me: 'Why are you going on? The Arab regimes are not going to help you. The governments of the world are not going to help you. Has anybody promised you anything? No. . . .'

. . . I said we owed it to future generations to stand and die if necessary. I said that if we gave up our struggle now, the spirit of Arab resistance would be crushed for ever.

Y. Arafat, quoted in Alan Hart, *Arafat: Terrorist or Peacemaker?*, Sidgwick & Jackson, 1984.

G   The Peace Plan of President Reagan

A British journalist comments on the plan.

On September 1 President Reagan made his plan public, calling for a freeze of Jewish settlements in occupied territories and offering Palestinians in Gaza and the West Bank their 'legitimate rights and just requirements' in a homeland to be associated with Jordan.

The President made no mention of the Palestine Liberation Organisation and he ruled out a Palestinian state. But in 'talking point' papers circulated by US embassies to selected Arab heads of state the phrase 'final outcome negotiable' appeared alongside many key points, including that of the status of a Palestinian **entity** on the West Bank.

The plan was a distinct move forward from the Camp David formula and by pointing to a Palestinian homeland in association with Jordan, President Reagan undercut Israel's idea of **fobbing off** the West Bank Palestinians with a limited **municipal authority**.

J. MacManus, 'Drawing a New Middle East Map', in the *Guardian*, 14 October 1982.

Glossary

abodes homes
conception creation
entity existence
exhorting strongly urging

fobbing off deceiving into accepting
municipal authority local government or town government

Questions

1 Read Sources A and F.
(a) What have the Palestinians been trying to achieve?
(b) What do they feel about their cause?
(c) Have they been realistic in their aims?
Give reasons for your answers.

2 Study Source B.
(a) What was the percentage increase in the number of Palestinian refugees from 1950 to 1968?

(Use the following formula: $\dfrac{\text{increase in number}}{\text{initial number}} \times 100$)

From your own knowledge explain the reasons for this increase.
(b) How do you explain the rise in the figures of refugees from 1967 to 1968?
(c) Which country had the largest number of Palestinian refugees in 1967? From your own knowledge explain how this caused a problem three years later.
(d) What percentage of the refugees in May 1967 were under fifteen? What problems do you think this caused?

3 Compare Sources C and D.
(a) What are the differences between these two extracts?
(b) How do you explain these differences?

4 Read Sources E(i), (ii) and (iii). Explain why:
(a) the number of terrorist incidents committed by Palestinians declined in the 1970s;
(b) E(ii) and (iii) give different views of the Munich assassinations.

5 Look at Sources D and F. Which speaker do you think was listened to most sympathetically in the West? Give reasons for your answer.

6 From the evidence in Source G draw a sketch-map fully labelled to show the various aspects of American plans for the Palestinians in 1982.

7 Using all the sources, give reasons why it is so difficult to draw up a peace plan which will be acceptable to both sides.

Chapter 24 Northern Ireland: the 'Troubles' since 1969

The majority of people in Northern Ireland want to live in peace. Yet since 1969 especially there has been much violence and bloodshed. The reasons are complex and have their roots deep in the past.

Introduction

In the seventeenth century Protestants from England and Scotland settled in the northern part of Ireland, the province of Ulster. The great majority of the Irish people were, as they still are, Roman Catholic. In 1688 the Catholic king of England, James II, was forced to leave the country and he was succeeded by his daughter Mary and her husband William, the Protestant Prince of Orange. James went to Ireland to raise a Catholic army but was defeated by William at the Battle of the Boyne. To this day William is a hero in the eyes of the Protestants of Northern Ireland, who formed an Orange Order pledged to keep Northern Ireland separate from the Catholic Irish Republic.

Ireland was partitioned in 1921. The bulk of the island became independent of Britain, while Northern Ireland remained part of the United Kingdom. However, the frontier was drawn in such a way that there were many Catholics in Northern Ireland. The Protestants controlled the area and discriminated against the Catholics who were not given equal opportunities for jobs, housing and representation in local government. Furthermore, many people in the Irish Republic felt that Ireland should be reunited – that Northern Ireland was a kind of British colony. The secret Irish Republican Army (IRA) was formed to 'win back' Northern Ireland from the British. In turn, the Protestants in Northern Ireland did not want to become part of a mainly Catholic united Ireland. They wanted to keep their union with Britain, and are therefore sometimes called 'Unionists' or 'Loyalists'.

Since 1969 the situation has been especially tense. After demonstrations in 1969 against the discriminatory laws and practices, violence became steadily worse with murder committed by both Protestants and Catholics. Although the laws were reformed it was too late; the IRA had seized its opportunity. The British government sent troops to try to keep the peace, but the IRA believed they were sent to reinforce British control.

A How the Roman Catholic minority has suffered

Discrimination against Catholics.

[In Derry, for example,] in 1966, the heads of all City Council departments were Protestant. Of 177 salaried employees, 145 – earning £124,424 – were Protestant, and only thirty-two – earning £20,420 – were Catholic.

But the big employers of labour were privately run companies, and although Catholics regularly suspected anti-Catholic prejudice among foremen or personnel managers, it is a hard thing to prove. All that can be recorded is that of 10,000 workers in the Belfast shipyard – the biggest single source of employment in the city – just 400 are Catholic.

But, as well as their role as employers, local councils are also big providers of housing; and housing is crucial. There are several ways in which Protestant councils have discriminated against Catholics. One has been to put Protestants in better houses than Catholics, but charge the same rents. . . . Another way has simply been to house more Protestants than Catholics.

The Sunday Times Insight Team, *Ulster*.

B   'How to make (the) Irish Stew'

The Sunday Times, 15 August 1971.

C   The police

(i) A statement by the Northern Ireland Prime Minister O'Neill, 5 January 1969, following disturbances in Londonderry on 1 January 1969.
  The 'Special Constabulary' were the 'B' Specials.

[The police] have handled this most difficult situation as fairly and as firmly as they could. . . .

But clearly Ulster has now had enough. We are all sick of marchers and counter-marchers. Unless these warring minorities rapidly return to their senses we will have to consider a further reinforcement of the regular police by greater use of the Special Constabulary for normal police duties.

Quoted in L. De Paor, *Divided Ulster*, Penguin, 1971.

(ii) Report of the Cameron Commission set up to investigate the communal tension and grievances in 1969.

Another matter of complaint which played a considerable part among the grievances felt particularly among the Catholic section of the community is the continued retention of the USC, commonly known as the ''B' Specials'. . . . The recruitment of this force, for traditional and historic reasons, is in practice limited to members of the Protestant faith. . . .

One very unfortunate consequence of these breaches of discipline, which occurred in predominantly Catholic areas of Londonderry and were directed against Catholic persons and property, was to add weight to the feeling which undoubtedly exists among a certain proportion of the Catholic community, that the police are biased in their conduct against Catholic demonstrations and demonstrators. Thus it is said that when the police have to interpose themselves between Unionist demonstrators on the one hand and a similar body of Catholic or Civil Rights demonstrators on the other, they invariably face the latter and have their backs to the former. The corollary is that if stones or other missiles are thrown from the Unionist crowd the police do not see who is responsible while they concentrate their attention against the non-Unionists. The fact is undoubted: the reason given for it – that Unionists being loyalists do not attack the police – is not accepted as satisfactory or a sufficient reply to the charge of partisan bias.

Disturbances in Northern Ireland, HMSO, 1969, quoted in J. Magee, *Northern Ireland, Crisis and Conflict*, Routledge & Kegan Paul, 1974.

(iii) Report of the Scarman Tribunal, investigating the disturbances of August 1969.
  'Civil rights activists' were people trying to obtain equal rights for Catholics in Northern Ireland.

It is painfully clear from the evidence **adduced** before us that by July the Catholic minority no longer believed that the RUC was impartial and that Catholic and civil rights activists were publicly asserting this loss of confidence. Understandably these resentments affected the thinking and feeling of the young and irresponsible, and induced the jeering and throwing of stones which were the small beginnings of most of the disturbances. The effect of this hostility on the RUC themselves was unfortunate. They came to treat as their enemies, and accordingly also as the enemies of the public peace, those who persisted in displaying hostility and distrust towards them.

Thus there developed the fateful split between the Catholic community and the police. Faced with the distrust of a substantial proportion of the whole population and short of numbers, the RUC had (as some senior officers appreciated) lost the capacity to control a major riot. Their difficulties naturally led them, when the emergency arose, to have recourse to methods such as baton-charges, CS gas and gunfire, which were ultimately to stoke even higher the fires of resentment and hatred.

Violence and Civil Disturbances in Northern Ireland in 1969, HMSO, 1972, quoted in Magee, *Northern Ireland, Crisis and Conflict*.

D   The Reverend Ian Paisley

Ian Paisley is the leader of the Democratic Unionist Party which wants to maintain the union with Britain.

'Fenians' were members of the nineteenth-century Irish Nationalist organisation, so Paisley's description of a 'Fenian Papist murderer' is a reference to this organisation and to the fact that Sean Lemass was a Catholic (Papist).

Underlying the scenes of violence of the past year is an earlier image: that of the Rev. Ian Paisley with his blackthorn stick, waiting in the streets of Armagh through the small hours of a November night in 1968 – while Protestants gathered to meet a Civil Rights march with billhooks, clubs, scythes and guns. . . .

Paisley's first political challenge came in 1956 when he accused O'Neill of betraying Unionism by entertaining at Stormont a 'Fenian Papist murderer' – a reference to the mild-mannered Irish Prime Minister, Sean Lemass, which astonished even many Unionists. Religion was Paisley's weapon. . . .

[Paisley] went to Rome himself in 1966 to protest against Archbishop Ramsey's visit to the Pope; a group who got in his way were later described as 'blaspheming, cursing, spitting, Roman scum.'

The Sunday Times Insight Team, *Ulster.*

E   'The Day Londonderry Exploded'

A British journalist describes the scene on the night before a Protestant march was to take place in August 1969.

Green is the symbolic colour of Irish nationalists (those who want to unite the whole of Ireland); hence the reference to the 'green giant'.

The 'Bogside' is a predominantly Catholic area of Londonderry.

Tensions had been heightening in Northern Ireland for ten months, ever since the RUC had brusquely water-cannoned a peaceful march against housing discrimination and so aroused the sullen green giant. . . .

On the Monday night, the Protestant **enclave** on the hill above the Bogside lit its traditional eve-of-march bonfires. The flames, the drifting sparks, and the accompanying jeering simply stoked up emotions below. That process continued on the Tuesday morning when tipsy Orangemen roamed the city walls throwing large, old-style pennies down at the Catholics.

But the activity on Monday night was far more frenzied within the Catholic enclave. I spent most of those small hours **circumspectly** crossing between Protestant and Catholic strongholds. The rollicking jollity of the Orange celebrants was in stark contrast to the grim scene in the Bogside.

There, large groups of men and youths were building barricades of rubble to seal off the streets, twisting roadside poles across the carriageway for the foundations. Around them, on the pavement outside the drab two-up-two-down houses, women, girls, and the younger boys were assembling petrol bombs.

A contemporary Irish joke centred on a reputed note for Bogside milkmen – 'Nothing today, but 150 empties please'. That night sustained the crack, and for weeks after the riots there was a chronic shortage of milk bottles.

Harold Jackson, 'The Day Londonderry Exploded', in the *Guardian*, 10 August 1984.

F   Violence

(i) A description by two journalists working on the *Belfast Telegraph.*

Provisional IRA leaders in Belfast and Dublin often do not know that their men were responsible for specific assassinations.

One example of this was the killing in January 1972 of the Protestant bus-driver, Sidney Agnew. A teenage boy and girl, both Provisional IRA

The 'Provisional IRA' is the more violent branch of the IRA. 'Brigade' and 'battalion' are levels of military command; brigade being higher.

volunteers, were ordered to kill Agnew, who was the principal prosecution witness against several IRA men charged with hijacking his corporation bus. The teenagers shot Agnew in front of his wife and children at his home in the Mount, in East Belfast. The decision to kill him had been taken at a meeting of the Ballymacarret Provisional IRA earlier in the evening. It was believed that if Agnew were killed and could not testify in court the following day, the accused would be able to leave court free. The Provisional brigade staff in Belfast, and the battalion staff covering the area, could not have been warned in advance that this decision had been taken. They would probably have been sufficiently aware of the law to know that as Agnew had already made **depositions** in court on oath about the incident these could be used at the trial if he was killed. Thus killing him was a futile act.

Martin Dillon and Denis Lehane, *Political Murder in Northern Ireland*, Penguin, 1973.

(ii) A speech by the Northern Ireland Prime Minister, Brian Faulkner, 24 January 1972.

We are speaking of hard-faced men. And I do not use that expression as an **epithet**, but as an accurate description of certain bitter and vicious countenances we have seen on public display – who shoot men in their own houses and before their own children; who place a deadly charge of high explosives next to an innocent victim in a pram; who drive a petrol-tanker with a booby-trap into a busy residential area; who shower a downtown shopping street with fragments of glass to tear the faces of women and young girls; who leave office-workers involved in a vital public service scarred and shattered; who break the knees of **confederates** whom they suspect of some offence against their code; who shave and tar young girls whose **heinous** offence is to love someone of whom they disapprove. That is real violence.

Quoted in Dillon and Lehane, *Political Murder in Northern Ireland*.

G A voice of the IRA

A statement by Sean Mac Stiofain, Chief of Staff of the Provisional IRA in 1972.
   'Stormont' Castle was where the Northern Ireland Parliament was situated.
   'Internees' are people who are in prison because they are suspected of being involved in terrorism.

In the end all loss of life in Northern Ireland rests with the Unionists, and with the British Government. They've brought the present situation about. We've given our terms for a truce.
   Our truce terms are: (1) That the British Army suspend all operations, withdraw from Catholic areas, pending their total withdrawal from the North. (2) That Stormont be abolished. (3) That a guarantee is given for the holding of free elections. (4) That all internees and political prisoners be released, North and South. (5) That compensation be paid to all those who've suffered as a result of British occupation. . . .
   There would be no place [in a United Ireland] for those who say they want their British heritage. They've got to accept their Irish heritage, and the Irish way of life, no matter who they are, otherwise there would be no place for them. . . . We say, first, you must get the British out, then it's up to us to ensure that we get a Socialist Republic, not a **'gombeen'** Republic.

Quoted in R. Sweetman, *On Our Knees*, Pan, 1972.

Glossary

adduced brought
circumspectly cautiously
confederates accomplices with the enemy
depositions written statements

enclave a territory surrounded by a foreign or alien power
epithet name, title
'gombeen' cheating, corrupt
heinous wicked

Questions

1 Read Source A and draw a diagram showing the ways in which the Protestants have been in control in Northern Ireland.

2 Look at Source B. Whom does the cartoonist blame for the troubles in Northern Ireland and for what reasons?

3 Compare Sources C(i), (ii) and (iii).
   (a) Who considers the police (i) most blameworthy; (ii) least blameworthy in provoking violence?
   (b) What, according to these sources, is the relationship between trust and law and order?
   (c) If you had been Prime Minister of Northern Ireland in 1972 what would you have done in the light of the Cameron and Scarman Reports? Give your reasons.

4 What does Source D tell you about the attitude of mind of Ian Paisley and his supporters in Northern Ireland? From your own knowledge explain how far this attitude has been justified.

5 Read Source E. How far do you think that the troubles which started in Northern Ireland in 1969 were caused by (a) fear and (b) historical memories?

6 Read Sources F(i) and (ii).
   (a) Describe the different views they give of terrorism.
   (b) How do you think the IRA justify the use of terrorism?

7 What do Sources D and G, taken together, tell you about the difficulties of finding a solution to the Northern Ireland problem?

Chapter 25 Great Britain: women's rights since the suffrage

Many women (and some men) argue that men still have too much control in public office and that women are unfairly discriminated against. How far have women in Britain succeeded in improving their status by political action in recent years?

Introduction

By 1884 all male householders in Britain had the right to vote in parliamentary elections. Yet women were still not allowed to vote. Women were also denied rights and privileges in many other areas – in education, employment, marriage and wages, for example. In 1903 Mrs Emmeline Pankhurst started a campaign to give women the vote, or suffrage as it was called. The women who took part in the campaign were called suffragettes and the struggle for the vote became extremely bitter. The First World War brought a halt to the campaign, but when many men were fighting in the army, women successfully took over their jobs – they became factory workers, farm workers and policewomen, for example. When the war ended in 1918, the government could no longer refuse; women over 30 were given the vote and from 1928, all women over 21 could vote.

But the vote did not mean that women were treated equally with men. For example, even as recently as the 1970s, there were so few women in 'top jobs' that when Mrs Thatcher became the first female leader of a British political party in 1975, the novelty caused considerable comment. As a result of this feeling of injustice, in the 1960s many women began to demand equal job opportunities and laws to prevent discrimination against women. The women's liberation movement which developed in the 1960s in Britain and other western countries went even further. They wanted to free women from a male-dominated society.

A Mrs Pankhurst's speech at Bow Street Court

In 1908 Mrs Pankhurst was brought before the court for her activities as a suffragette. She made this speech from the dock.

'Seven and sixpence' in decimal money is 37½ pence. By way of comparison, the old age pension in 1908 was the equivalent of 25 pence.

We believe that if we get the vote it will mean better conditions for our unfortunate sisters. Many women pass through this court who would not come before you if they were able to live morally and honestly. The average earnings of the women who earn their living in this country are only seven and sixpence a week. Some of us have worked for many years to help our own sex, and we have been driven to the conclusion that only through legislation can any improvement be effected, and that the legislation can never be **effected** until we have the same power as men to bring pressure to bear upon governments to give us the necessary legislation. . . .

No, sir, I do say deliberately to you that I come here not as an ordinary law-breaker. I should never be here if I had the same kind of laws that the very meanest and commonest of men have – the same power that the wife-beater has, the same power that the drunkard has. This is the only way we have to get that power which every citizen should have of deciding how the taxes she contributes to should be made, and until we get that power we shall be here. . . .

We are not here because we are law-breakers, we are here in our efforts to become law-*makers!*

Quoted in L. Baily, *B.B.C. Scrapbook I*, BBC Publications, 1966.

B   A male comment about the first woman MP

Sixty years ago . . . the male **monopoly** of parliament was broken when the first woman MP took her seat in the House of Commons. Ten years later there was a woman Cabinet Minister, and now we have a woman Prime Minister. All things considered, women have advanced very rapidly in British politics since 1 December 1919, and all who believe in sexual equality should be grateful to the woman who achieved the historic breakthrough – Nancy Astor . . . [In 1946 her husband] decided it was essential for her to withdraw. His health had collapsed and he knew that he would not be able to help her, as in the past. So just before the twenty-fifth anniversary of her entry into parliament he wrote to the Divisional Tories to say that she would not be standing again.

John Grigg, *The Observer*, 25 November 1979.

C   Women in important positions

(i) Maureen Colquhoun speaking in the House of Commons on her Private Member's Bill on the Balance of the Sexes, May 1965.

The Covent Garden Market Authority has six men, no women. I do not know whether that authority was responsible for the environmental damage in Covent Garden. If so, it might well have been improved with some women on the board.

The National Bus Company has seven men, no women. Of course, women do not travel on buses. Neither, apparently, do they travel on trains, because the British Railways Board has 12 men, no women.

What about the 14 male members of the Building Research Establishment Advisory Committee? Surely they need a little help from their friends. I suspect that there is one thing we can say for them. They obviously do not believe that a woman's place is in the home.

Among the 24 members of the Advisory Panel on Arms Control and Disarmament there are no women appointed, yet surely disarmament and arms control is a subject very much of interest to women. They ought to be there and they ought to be having a say. Or does the world of men still believe that 'They also serve who only stand and wait'?

I must confess that all is not entirely bleak. I was delighted with the appointments made by my right hon. Friend the Secretary of State for Prices and Consumer Protection, whose Department has just set up the National Consumer Council with 13 women and five men. That is something for the Guinness Book of Records. I suspect that it is the only Government-appointed body with a majority of women.

Quoted in I. Reid and E. Wormald (eds.), *Sex Differences in Britain*, Grant McIntyre, 1982.

(ii) Appointments to public bodies, 1983.

Parent Department	No. of bodies to which appointments made	Male appointments	Female appointments	Women as a percentage of total
Scottish Office[1]	229	3,095	1,319	29.9
Home Office[1]	241	2,499	1,023	29.0
Trade and Industry[1]	104	1,057	320	23.2
Health and Social Security	165	9,606	2,840	22.8
Environment	186	6,158	966	13.6
Employment	228	5,329	806	13.1
Education and Science	30	661	85	11.4
Welsh Office	48	813	94	10.4
Transport	28	385	34	8.1
Foreign and Commonwealth Office	29	288	23	7.4
Energy	23	211	16	7.0
Inland Revenue and HM Customs and Excise	4	5,206	282	5.1
Defence	51	409	18	4.2
Agriculture, Fisheries and Food	106	1,481	50	3.3
HM Treasury	11	91	3	3.2
Total	1,483	37,289	7,879	17.4

Notes:
[1] Sex of some appointees is not known; these are therefore excluded from this analysis.
Source: Compiled from Management and Personnel Office, *Public Bodies 1983*, HMSO.

D Women in parliament

(i) Percentage of women parliamentary members: General Elections 1918–79.

Year	Cons.	Lab.	Lib.	Others	All parties
1918	0.0	0.0	0.0	0.9	0.1
1922	0.3	0.0	0.9	0.0	0.3
1923	1.2	1.6	1.3	0.0	1.3
1924	0.7	0.7	0.0	0.0	0.7
1929	1.2	3.1	1.7	11.1	2.3
1931	2.5	0.0	2.7	20.0	2.4
1935	1.4	0.6	4.8	9.1	1.5
1945	0.5	5.3	8.3	4.0	3.8
1950	2.0	4.4	11.1	0.0	3.4
1951	1.9	3.7	0.0	0.0	2.7
1955	2.9	5.0	0.0	0.0	3.8
1959	3.3	5.0	0.0	0.0	4.0
1964	3.6	5.7	0.0	0.0	4.6
1966	2.8	5.2	0.0	0.0	4.1
1970	4.5	3.5	0.0	14.3	4.1
1974 Feb.	3.0	4.3	0.0	4.3	3.6
1974 Oct.	2.5	5.6	0.0	7.7	4.2
1979	2.4	4.1	0.0	0.0	3.0
1983	3.3	7.3	0.0	0.0	4.6

M. Stacey and M. Price, *Women, Power and Politics*, Tavistock, 1981.

(ii) The lack of women MPs.

Since women over thirty first got the vote in 1918 they have encouraged much wider subjects for parliamentary debate, including welfare, health, social services, abortion and divorce; but they have had much less effect on the make-up of the House. . . . The lack of women is largely due to their difficulties in taking the job; as Shirley Williams has complained: 'Look back on the women MPs of a generation ago; a very high proportion were single or widowed, some succeeding their deceased husbands for the same constituency. Of today's women MPs and candidates, many are trying to keep a family and a job going at the same time. Parliament's timetable ensures that any reasonably responsible parent will live in a perpetual state of mild guilt. . . .'

Anthony Sampson, *The Changing Anatomy of Britain*, Coronet Books, 1983. The quotation from Mrs Williams is from the *Guardian*, 30 October 1979.

E Party manifestos

(i) Conservative Party Manifesto, October 1974.

Women – at home and at work

Child credits for Mothers
. . . we plan as part of our tax credit scheme to introduce new child credits for all children, including the first. These will be worth more than the existing family allowances. . . .

Women at Work
. . . We stand by the principle of equal pay for women.

Women in Retirement
Women have had a rough deal over pensions from the present government, which has abandoned the last Conservative government's Second Pension Scheme. . . . A Conservative government will reintroduce the scheme.

Widows
In relation to supplementary benefit, we also intend, as we have said, to relax the earnings rule so as to enable widows to make a real contribution to the living standards of their families.

The Right of a Woman to be Treated Equally
The last Conservative government made considerable progress in strengthening women's rights. In pensions, social benefits, taxation, maintenance payments and guardianship of children, we introduced a succession of new rights for women. We also announced our intention to set up an Equal Opportunities Commission, the biggest single step towards a society of real equality for men and women taken by any government since women won the vote. Only the timing of the election prevented its implementation. We remain committed to setting up an Equal Opportunities Commission with powers to enquire into areas of discrimination and to report to the Government on the need for future action.

Putting Britain First, the Conservative Party Manifesto for the election of October 1974.

(ii) Labour Party Manifesto, October 1974.

A 'White Paper' is a pamphlet announcing proposed legislation.

A CHARTER FOR WOMEN

. . . The Labour Government's decisions provide a new deal for women. We will:
* ensure that by the end of 1975 Labour's Equal Pay Act will be fully effective throughout the land;
* introduce a comprehensive free family planning service;
* legislate for equality of treatment in social security;
* make provision for maternity leave;

* introduce a new child cash allowance to be paid (including the first child) usually to mothers;
* extend nursery education and day care facilities;
* bring a fairer system of family law with new family courts;
* reform housing law, to strengthen the rights of mothers on the break-up of marriage: and introduce other reforms proposed by the Finer Committee on One Parent Families;
* increase educational opportunities for girls, including further education, training and compulsory day release.

We also intend to legislate directly on new rights for women, through a Sex Discrimination Bill as set out in our White Paper. The proposals cover: employment, training, education, housing and the provision of goods, facilities and services (including mortgages and H.P., etc.). There will also be new machinery to ensure the enforcement of these measures. But of course all our proposals – about prices and consumer protection and homes and education and full employment – will help to improve life for all the women of our country. And we are determined to see more of them from all walks of life – in Parliament, on local councils and other public bodies – including political parties and trade union committees.

Britain Will Win With Labour, the Labour Party Manifesto for the election of October 1974.

F New laws are not good enough

A female journalist writing in a national newspaper.

If progress towards equality was measured in neat legal packages, we'd have come a long way since 1974. But how much difference have all these new 'rights' made to women's lives? The Social Security Act 1975 does not protect the pension rights of women with home responsibilities, unless they are single parents. . . . The new provisions for maternity leave will be of little use to most women. Those who manage to fulfil the tough qualifying conditions will benefit only if they can find somewhere suitable to leave their children when they return to work. Nursery facilities are notoriously scarce – . . .

The weaknesses of the Sex Discrimination Act are already well known. Constructed in response to a vigorous campaign and launched on a tide of optimism it has proved leaky and unmanoeuvrable. We are still waiting for the Equal Opportunities Commission to justify its existence.

So for all our new rights we have made very little progress in three and a half years. Women's average earnings are still less than 60 per cent of men's. Most women remain in lower paid 'women's jobs' where they have no chance of claiming equal pay. Few benefit from apprenticeship or day-release training. Women still do most or all of the domestic chores whether or not they have full-time jobs. Many **overt** and legal terms of discrimination persist.

Anna Coote, 'Legal rights are one thing' in the *Guardian*, 22 August 1977.

G Press reporting

Ann Oakley commenting on the media coverage of a major women's event.

In 1970 the British women's liberation movement held its first national conference in Oxford. *Shrew*, the magazine of the women's liberation work-shop, analysed media reports of the conference. *The Observer*'s reporter

The *'Thoughts of Chairman Mao'* is a book of revolutionary sayings and advice by the Chinese leader.

described its participants as 'young, violent, radical and very attractive with their long hair and maxi-coats', and mentioned that the bookstall sold the *Thoughts of Chairman Mao*. '**Militancy** in the kitchen' was the heading of the *Times* report; the *Guardian*, which devoted only 4½ inches to their report, included one sentence describing the content of the conference. In *The Daily Telegraph* prominence was given to the heckling and call for order ('Squabbling as women talk of liberation'). . . .

The concentration on details of appearance, on unrepresentative themes and moments of disorganization, conveys a scene of silly schoolgirls thoughtlessly engaging in an act of mild **sabotage**. No one would guess from this report that ten years later the women's movement would still be going strong. . . .

Whatever else feminist politics have done in the last decade, they have broadened the concept of the political. . . . Politics, in any and every sense, is about power, and it is as much about the power that men, wittingly or unwittingly, exercise over women as it is about the power that presidents and prime ministers wield over nations.

Ann Oakley, *Subject Women*, Fontana, 1982.

Glossary

effected	brought about	**overt**	unconcealed, obvious
militancy	fighting for their rights	**sabotage**	intentional damage
monopoly	control by one group		

Questions

1   Compare Sources B, D(i) and D(ii).
   (a) What do the circumstances surrounding Lady Astor's retirement from parliament (Source B) tell you about the position of women in politics in the 1940s?
   (b) How far do you agree with John Grigg's statement that, 'All things considered, women have advanced very rapidly in British politics since 1 December 1919'?

2   Study Sources C(i) and (ii).
   (a) For what kinds of jobs are women thought to be most and least suitable?
   (b) Do you think that these views are accurate and just?
   Give reasons for your answers.

3   Read Sources E(i) and (ii).
   (a) If you had the vote in 1974 and wished to use it to support improvements for the condition of women, for which party would you have voted? Explain the reasons for your decision.
   (b) From your own knowledge state which party won the election in October 1974.
   (c) Which manifesto, Source E(i) or E(ii), was therefore the basis of government policy from 1974?
   (d) Compare the extract from that manifesto with Source F and explain how far the government had honoured its promises by 1977.

4   Study Source A.
   (a) Mrs Pankhurst believes two changes will improve conditions for women. What are they?
   (b) Do the other sources confirm her belief? Give reasons for your answer.

5   Compare Sources A and G. What evidence do they provide about attitudes towards the women's movement in 1908 and 1970?